AN IRISH CENTURY
1845 ∽ 1945

FROM THE FAMINE
TO THE END OF WORLD WAR II

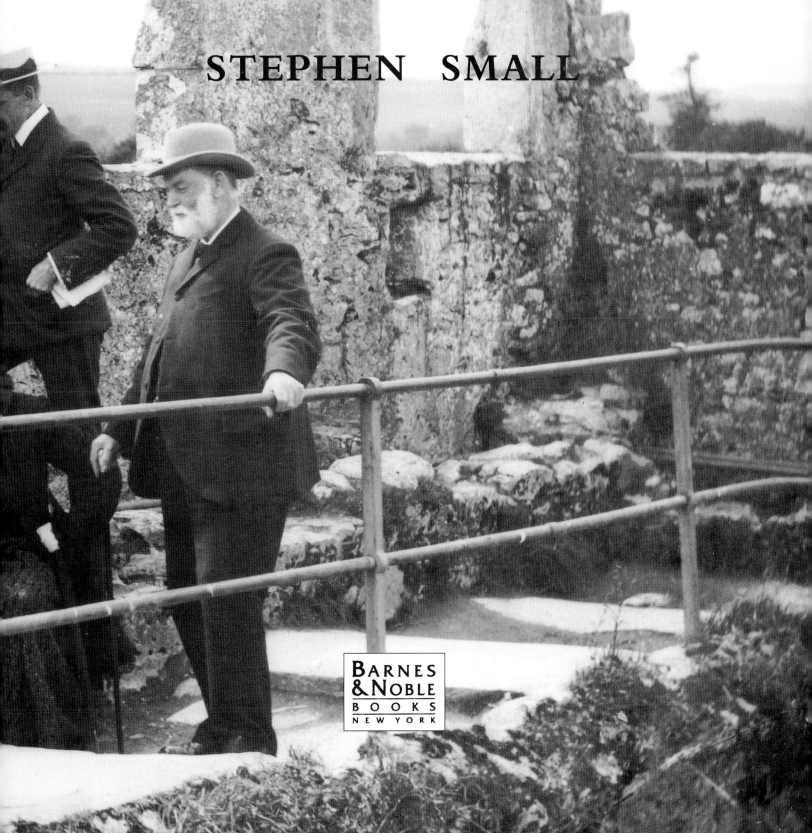

AN IRISH CENTURY
1845 ∽ 1945

FROM THE FAMINE
TO THE END OF WORLD WAR II

STEPHEN SMALL

BARNES
&NOBLE
BOOKS
NEW YORK

Dedication
This book is dedicated to the budding scholar Joseph Solomon Small.

ACKNOWLEDGMENTS

To acknowledge all the historians whose work has influenced this book would require a detailed bibliography inappropriate to such a work. However, the author would like to pay particular tribute to J. C. Beckett, R. F. Foster, J. J. Lee and F. S. L. Lyons, and happily direct readers interested in delving deeper into Irish history to their work.

He would like to thank his wife Millicent and his parents for their love and support over the past year.

The Author and Publisher would like gratefully to acknowledge the assistance of the following organisations for the photographs listed below:

Kilmainham Gaol
Cover (portrait of Parnell), 40, 42, 43, 44, 46, 48, 47, 52, 53(B), 54, 71, 72, 73, 74(T, A), 75 (BR), 76(TL, TR), 77, 78, 79(TL, B), 152(B), 173, 175. Much of the material from Kilmainham Gaol can be seen in the excellent Document Packs for Secondary Schools on Kilmainham Gaol produced by the Office of Public Works and Blackrock Teachers' Centre

Bord Fáilte/Irish Tourist Board
Back cover, 6/7, 8, 9, 17, 21, 22, 23(L), 65(TL), 79(TR), 85(T), 112/113, 115, 116, 117, 118, 119, 120/121, 122, 123, 124, 125, 126(T), 127, 128, 129, 130, 131, 132, 133, 140, 141, 144(B), 145, 146, 147, 148/149, 150, 151, 152(T), 157, 158, 160(B), 166/167, 168, 170(T), 171, 172, 176(T), 177, 178, 182, 183, 184/185, 190

via Harland and Wolff
Photographs reproduced by kind permission of the Trustees of the Ulster Museum: 35, 36/37, 114, 138(B), 139(B), 142, 181

National Library of Ireland
Cover (main picture), 2/3, 10, 11, 13, 14, 15, 18/19, 20, 24, 25, 26, 27, 28, 29, 30, 31, 32, 33, 38, 39, 41, 45, 47, 49, 50/51, 53(T), 54, 55, 56, 58, 59, 60, 61, 62, 63, 64, 65(TR, B), 66, 67, 70, 74(C), 75(L, T), 76(B), 81, 82, 83, 84, 85(B), 86, 87, 88, 89, 90, 93(T), 98, 102, 103, 104, 105, 106, 107, 108, 126(B), 134, 135, 136, 137, 138(T), 139(T, C), 144(T), 146(TR, TL), 153, 156, 159, 160(T), 161, 162, 163, 164, 165, 170(B), 174, 176(B), 179

Barnaby's Picture Library
23(R), 69, 96, 99(T), 100, 110/111, 154(T), 155

Hulton Getty Collection
91, 93(B), 97, 99 (B), 101, 154(B), 169,

BPL
Cover (Michael Collins), 80, 94/95, 99, 109

PREVIOUS PAGE: Early 20th century tourists at Blarney Castle, Co. Cork, follow the tradition of kissing the Blarney Stone in the hope of gaining "the gift of the gab."

This edition published 1998 by Barnes and Noble Inc., by arrangement with PRC Publishing Ltd

Produced by PRC Publishing Ltd
Kiln House, 210 New Kings Road
London SW6 4NZ

© 1998 PRC Publishing Ltd

ISBN 0-76070-879-7

Printed in China
M 10 9 8 7 6 5 4 3 2 1

CONTENTS

INTRODUCTION

PREVIOUS PAGE: Two Aran islanders sheep shearing — a timeless scene which would have been familiar to J. M. Synge, who immortalized these barren islands off the west coast of Ireland in a series of brilliant and controversial plays produced for the Abbey Theatre. The most notable was The Playboy of the Western World, *which caused riots after its first performance in 1907.*

ABOVE and RIGHT: Peat, or turf, was a vital part of the Irish rural economy for centuries. Not only was it used as a low grade fuel which filled windowless cabins with a red, smoky, fire, it was also used as a building material. In a land with no coal and, in some areas, very little timber, peat was the only fuel most families had.

The history of Ireland is most often seen as a history of national struggle. The dominant theme is the relationship of Ireland to Britain, and attempts to change that relationship are its variations. As a model for understanding the political, economic, social and cultural life of Ireland, this framework has its value — especially in the century covered by this book. Young Ireland, the Fenians, the IRB, the Land League, Parnell, the Home Rule party, Sinn Fein and the IRA were the very stuff of Irish national life. In completely different ways, all of them were motivated by opinions about the relationship between Ireland and Britain. These opinions undoubtedly focused the energies and intellects of many Irish men and women, and the activity that flowed from them will form an important part of the story that follows. However, for two reasons this model does not tell the whole story.

Firstly, the conflicts, loyalties and political interests of the Irish people have always been diverse and changeable. Apart from the most obvious divisions between Catholic and Protestant, Nationalist and Unionist, the island of Ireland has contained a wide variety of ethnic and religious groupings and a continually evolving set of identities and allegiances. The course of Irish history has never been as straightforward a struggle for independence as some historians would have us believe. Secondly, this framework obscures the day-to-day existence of ordinary Irish people. The more private world of family, work, leisure and religion usually loomed larger in most people's minds than struggles for political rights, and the harsh realities of poverty and emigration were often more pressing than national self-determination — however strongly many people felt about it. In a book such as this, which tries to capture the flavor of Irish life through photographs of everyday scenes, of ordinary people at work and at play, of life on the farm and life in the city these everyday concerns should not be forgotten.

It is all too easy to see history as, simply, the story of great men and women, of great political events, of kings and queens, wars and battles, heroes and villains. Most of the people living through great events are indeed aware of them but — unless put in a life-threatening position —are more aware of more urgent problems. In the mid-19th century, Ireland was in a catastrophic condition. Five years of famine had caused a million to die from hunger and disease, and well over a million to emigrate. In many areas of the west and south the social and economic fabric of the country was in tatters. The inhabitants of Ireland were more concerned about where their next meal was to come from than anything else. But the effects of the great famine did have an effect on both people's political viewpoint as well as their numbers. Undoubtedly the middle of the 19th century was a major turning point in Irish history, for mentally and physically a very different country would emerge after this date.

In order to gain a clearer picture of these changes and their significance, we need to examine what kind of country Ireland was before the famine and briefly recount the

events that led up to it. For not everything changed, and those changes that did take place were shaped by what had gone before.

Geography and history are always intertwined, and this is the case with Ireland more than with most countries. It sits off the north-western fringe of Europe as the second largest in a group of relatively small islands, and its history has been defined by two inescapable relationships arising from this geography: its distance from the early origins of western civilization, and its proximity to the larger island in its group — Britain. Ireland's place on the edge of Europe meant that until relatively recently it was usually (although by no means always) distanced from the main currents of European and world history. This had both positive and negative effects. Ireland was often late in adopting newer and more efficient modes of living, and as a result has usually been poorer than its nearest neighbors, but its remoteness also allowed cultures to flourish long after they had been destroyed in the more accessible parts of Europe — protecting vital elements of ancient learning and civilization in periods of general upheaval and disorder.

Ireland's other inescapable geographical fact, its closeness to Britain, has also been a very mixed blessing. Britain has been a link between Ireland and Europe for peoples and ideas, as well as a source of modernizing energy in its own right, but the various peoples of Britain have imposed their own cultural, legal and economic systems on Ireland in a way that was often extremely painful for its existing inhabitants. The varying nature of these influences and impositions will be examined later, but it is sufficient to note here that Ireland's location made it unable to avoid the considerable trauma of being neighbor to an increasingly powerful state. From the 16th century until the 19th, England, and then Britain, gradually developed into the world's most powerful nation, and its strategic, religious and economic interests affected Ireland profoundly.

IRELAND BEFORE THE ACT OF UNION

Before the invasion of Anglo-Norman settlers from England and Wales in the late 12th century, new technologies, materials and peoples reached Ireland gradually as they spread out from the cradle of civilization in the Middle East. Ireland's first inhabitants arrived via Britain around 6,000BC; they scratched a living hunting and fishing in the virgin forests, lakes and rivers. By 3,000BC the first farmers reached Ireland. This culture, known for its incredible megalithic (meaning large stone) tombs like Newgrange, has left its physical marks on the Irish landscape. By 2,000BC a new wave of settlers with Bronze Age techniques of metalworking were dominant in Ireland. Irish copper and gold attracted traders and colonizers from all over Europe, including the Celts. From about 600BC, Celtic peoples began to invade Ireland and by around 150BC they established a dominance based on their superior iron technology.

The Celts brought with them the characteristic visual imagery which is now iconic of ancient Irish culture. Their jewelry and weapons were adorned with intricate, swirling patterns — the extended limbs of dragons and other beasts interlocking with beautiful geometric

designs. This flourishing culture also provided the myths and legends which proved inspirational to 19th century Irish writers of the cultural revival. The most famous of these chronicles, the Fionn Cycle and the Tain Bo Cuailnge (Cattle Raid of Cooley), depicted the courageous feats of archetypal Irish warrior heroes, such as Cuchulain (pronounced Koohulann) and left a lasting imprint on Irish minds.

When Christianity was established in Ireland in the 5th century AD, largely through the efforts of the Celtic Briton St. Patrick, it merged with these older Celtic traditions; but once again Ireland's place on the edge of Europe gave this latest cultural import a distinctive difference. Unlike most of western Europe (including most of Britain), Ireland was never conquered by the Romans. There is some evidence of a Roman settlement on the eastern coast of Ireland but the island was never part of the Roman Empire. Hence Ireland developed a unique Celtic Christianity rather than adopting the Romanized form taken by the rest of western Europe. When the Roman Empire collapsed under the weight of barbarian invasions during the 5th century AD, the position of Ireland allowed it to become a remote repository of knowledge in troubled times.

For hundreds of years after this collapse (the so-called "Dark Ages") the Irish monasteries maintained vital elements of Christian learning which had been wiped out in most of western Europe. Irish missionaries such as St. Columba and St. Columbanus became famous for their learning throughout Europe. From their monasteries at Bangor, on Iona (off western Scotland), and on

ABOVE LEFT: New meets old on Patrick Street in turn-of-the-century Cork. The modernization of Ireland which took place between 1845 and 1945 is encapsulated in the trams jostling for space with horse-drawn carriages.

ABOVE: A group of poor Connemara peasants ascend the valley of Lough Nafooey in Co. Galway. This impoverished area was one of the worst affected by the famine and its lifestyle changed little from ancient times until quite recently.

Lindisfarne (off north-eastern England), they helped to convert to Christianity many of the Germanic and Slavic tribes which had invaded the Roman Empire. Many of the newly-settled colonizers of what is now Britain, France, Switzerland and much of Germany owed their conversion to Irish monks. One Irish monk, Virgil of Salzburg, even converted Slavic tribes as far away as Moravia.

Due to Ireland's place at the edge of Europe, this Celtic Christian culture survived largely unmolested until the Viking incursions which began in 795AD. Even after the Anglo-Norman settlers began to arrive after 1170, it remained dominant in much of Ireland right up to the 17th century — and beyond in remote western areas. Its high standing crosses, round towers and monasteries became such a strong part of the Irish consciousness that they remain among the most powerful visual evocations of Ireland and this tradition gave the Irish Celts a unified language and culture.

Celtic Ireland was ruled by chieftains who, occasionally, could find enough cross-clan support to be called

"High King". The most famous of the Celtic high kings was Brian Boru (Bhriain Boroimh) of Munster, who briefly united Ireland by a decisive victory over a mixed force of Leinster Celts and Vikings at Clontarf in 1014. For the next 150 years the Celts held sway in Ireland, but tribal rivalry continued. When Dermot MacMurrough of Leinster, invited the Anglo-Norman noble, Richard de Clare, Earl of Pembroke (also known as Strongbow) to help him regain his lands in 1167, Irish history entered a new phase.

From this point the second of our two geographical facts becomes more important. We should note immediately that these colonizers were not "English" or "British" in a modern sense. They were the recent descendants of Norman nobles who had accompanied William the Conqueror in his invasion of England from northern France barely a century before. They swiftly established themselves in Ireland and this effectively established the rule of the English crown. For although Strongbow married MacMurrough's daughter and set himself up as King of Leinster after his death, Strongbow himself owed allegiance to Henry II, who was king of England, as well as much of France. Henry had no desire to see a strong new kingdom emerge on his western flank under one of his own vassals, and so he came to Ireland himself in 1171 to demand allegiance from Strongbow as well as the major Irish and Viking leaders. In doing so he established a permanent English presence in Ireland.

Within 80 years the Normans had established in much of Ireland the feudal structures and laws current in England, controlling most of the land, but until the efforts of Henry VIII and Elizabeth I in Tudor times, this "English" conquest of Ireland was always somewhat haphazard. The initial achievement of a handful of nobles was remarkable as they had very little help from the English crown, but they tended only to occupy the river valleys, plains and coasts, leaving the hills, bogs, and forests to the native Celts. Trade and agriculture flourished in those areas under Norman rule, but life outside their new towns retained its traditional Celtic flavor. Indeed many Norman colonists, who were always heavily outnumbered by the Gaelic Celts, soon began to adopt the Gaelic customs and language. As the Norman nobility intermarried with the Gaelic nobility, Gaelic chieftains slowly regained much of their power, and this encouraged a flowering Gaelic history and poetry.

During the 14th and 15th centuries effective English control dwindled to a small area on Ireland's eastern coast around Dublin, known as "the Pale." Many of these "Old English" (as the Normans came to be known) became so immersed in Gaelic ways that the English crown began to lose control over them. The fear that the descendants of the Norman settlers were "becoming more Irish than the Irish" led the Irish Parliament to introduce a set of laws in 1366 forbidding the Old English from using the Gaelic customs, laws and language. These laws, known as the Statutes of Kilkenny, should be seen as an attempt to keep the Old English in line, rather than to persecute the Gaelic Irish. They are remarkable as perhaps the first known attempt at formal apartheid in history.

In the 16th century the vigorous Tudor monarchs, especially Henry VIII, embarked on a program of reconquest. All nobles would acknowledge his supremacy by surrendering their lands to the crown, and then have them granted back to them as feudal lordships — in effect, turning Irish chiefs into English nobles. For the Old English in Ireland this was merely a restatement of their formal position. For the Gaelic chiefs it represented the destruction of their customary power and was incompatible with their understanding of land ownership. In Brehon law, unlike English law, the land was owned by the clan and not the current chief. So even if one Irish chief agreed to surrender the lands of his clan, his successor could justifiably claim the land back on the grounds that it had never been within the rights of the last chief to give it away.

The bitterness of these conflicts was greatly heightened by a new animosity in Anglo-Irish relations — religion. The reformation had turned England into a largely Protestant country, but it had barely touched Ireland outside the Pale. The common Catholicism of the Gaelic and Old English nobles often led to joint resistance as the English attempted to impose their Protestant faith alongside their political control. While religion helped to unite different kinds of Irishmen, it made Irish reconquest seem imperative for England. In Elizabeth's time, England saw itself as surrounded by powerful Catholic enemies in France and Spain — England's narrow escape from invasion by the Spanish Armada in 1588 demonstrated that a Catholic Ireland allied to Spain could be disastrous for England's safety.

The old world of independent Gaelic kingship finally disappeared in battles with the Tudor monarchs. As a result, effective English control of the whole of Ireland was achieved for first time. In 1607, still broken by their humiliation and fearful of persecution, around 90 of Ulster's traditional Gaelic Catholic elite abandoned their lands and left for France. This desertion, the famous "Flight of the Earls," left Ulster, traditionally the least manageable province of all Ireland, open to the Protestant colonization (or "plantations") which have been the cause of so much of Ireland's tensions. The subsequent influx of state-sponsored Protestant settlers was not confined to the Ulster counties. Tyrone, Armagh, Donegal, Fermanagh, Cavan and Coleraine (which, with additions from Tyrone, became Londonderry) saw extensive and enduring colonization, but British Protestants settled all over Ireland. The most successful were the Presbyterians, who settled in the east of Ulster with little help from the crown. They made the short crossing from

ABOVE RIGHT: The General Post Office on Sackville Street (now O'Connell Street) in Dublin has a special place in Irish history. It was used by the insurgents as their headquarters during the Easter Rising, and you can still see the filled-in bullet holes to this day.

BELOW RIGHT: By the end of our period buses and motor cars were beginning to transform Irish life. This photograph of Patrick Street in Cork in the 1940s provides an interesting contrast with that on page 10.

ABOVE: William of Orange crosses the Boyne after his victory over James II in 1690. This battle helped to establish Protestant hegemony in Ireland and has become a vital part of Protestant folk memory. Its anniversary on July 12 is still commemorated with vigor by the Orangemen of Northern Ireland.

Scotland largely by their own initiative and created a solid Presbyterian heartland in Antrim and Down.

Over the 17th century the bulk of all Irish land changed hands, from Old English and Gaelic Catholics to new English and Scottish Protestants. This shift of power and wealth was the outcome of a century of war and upheaval on a grand scale, as Ireland became caught up in the wider conflicts of British and European power politics. The two key episodes were Ireland's involvement in the civil wars which racked the British Isles between 1639 and 1652, and William III's "Glorious Revolution" of 1688–91.

At the start of the Civil War, the Confederation of Kilkenny (as the Irish Catholic alliance became known) realized they would suffer a far worse fate if the zealous anti-Catholic puritans of the English parliament defeated Charles I. For eight years a confusing array of English, Scottish and Irish armies caused immeasurable suffering until Charles's defeat in England by Cromwell allowed the Parliamentary armies to devote their full attention to Ireland. Few episodes in Irish history are as notorious as Cromwell's punitive campaign of 1649. After massacres at Drogheda and Wexford, his forces swiftly reduced Irish resistance. His victory was followed by the largest single

dispossession of Catholics in Irish history. Unable to pay his army with money, thousands of his English and Scottish soldiers were rewarded with grants of land confiscated from their defeated enemies. The scale of this transfer of land was enormous. Before Cromwell's intervention, Catholics had still held about 60 percent of the land; by the time of the restoration of Charles II in 1660, this figure was probably nearer 20 percent.

Protestant dominance was further reinforced toward the end of the century as a result of the "Glorious Revolution." In 1685 James II, a Catholic, had become king of England, Scotland and Ireland, and in 1688 his second wife surprisingly produced a male heir. The prospect of a permanent Catholic dynasty was so disturbing for the English Protestant elite that a group of nobles invited Mary (James's Protestant daughter from his first marriage) to take the throne with her husband William of Orange.

William defeated James's armies at the battles of the Boyne in 1690, and Aughrim and Limerick in 1691 to secure Protestant dominance in Ireland — and Protestant Ireland set about securing its land and political privileges with vigor. Religion, rather than ethnicity, was now the defining feature of Ireland, and over the next generation, the Irish parliament passed a set of laws which discriminated against Catholics in almost every sphere of life. In flagrant breach of the treaty of Limerick, Catholics were excluded from voting or sitting in parliament, and from educating their young in Ireland. Mixed marriages were illegal and powerful incentives were given to those who

ABOVE: *Guards on parade at Dublin Castle, the bastion of British rule in Ireland. This building became so closely associated with the government in the popular mind that "the Castle" became a universal synonym for the British administration in Ireland.*

would convert to the legally established Protestant Church of Ireland. Toleration of Catholics increased in the late 18th century and, as Protestants began to feel more secure and prosperous, they began to develop a greater sense of their own identity and independence. This new Irish patriotism, or "colonial nationalism" as it is sometimes called, had much in common with the American patriotism which led to the American Revolutionary War. A frustration with British interference in Irish political and commercial affairs led to the growth of a movement known as the Volunteers. Initially this was a home defence force set up to protect Ireland from French invasion during the American Revolutionary War, but the volunteers quickly acquired a radical political role. They used Britain's difficulties in America to demand free trade and legislative independence for their parliament. By 1782, the British Parliament had been forced to renounce its right to make laws for Ireland and (with a few exceptions) to control Irish trade with other countries. The newly "independent" Irish Parliament became known as Grattan's Parliament, after the Protestant patriot leader whose oratory was instrumental in forcing these victories, but in reality little changed. The head of state of both countries was still George III, and his ministers were still able to manipulate the Irish Parliament through the distribution of well-paid government jobs and pensions.

By 1793 Catholics had been given the vote again, and most of the penal laws had been repealed, but they were still not allowed to sit in parliament and the Irish government remained exclusively Protestant and very aristocratic. A United Irish rebellion finally exploded in Wexford and north-east Ulster in 1798. United Irish leaders, such as Wolfe Tone, were usually middle-class Protestants who professed enlightened toleration of all religions and the equal rights of all Irish citizens, but the rebellion took on a sectarian character. This was especially the case in Wexford, where the most serious fighting took place. After some initial success, the poorly armed and organized army of peasants was decimated at Vinegar Hill. At least 30,000 were killed during the rebellion, which finally convinced the British government that direct rule from Britain was necessary. The Irish Parliament was bribed and cajoled into voting for its own dissolution, and in 1801 the Act of Union came into effect.

FROM THE ACT OF UNION TO THE FAMINE

The rebellion and Union left a bitter legacy which defined the religious and political allegiances that persist in Ireland to this day. Although many Protestants were initially against the Union, it rapidly became seen as their best protection against future outbreaks of Catholic violence. Conversely, many Catholics had supported the Union at the time, partly because they were promised emancipation as part of the deal; partly because the Protestant Ascendancy in Ireland had proved itself a far greater enemy to Catholic rights than the British government. But George III opposed the attempt to bring in a bill for emancipation, and this made it unlikely that Catholics would become reconciled to the Union. By the 1820s and 1830s a number of factors contributed to a growing sense of resentment among Catholics. Firstly, an agricultural slump after the Napoleonic Wars caused great poverty among an expanding peasant class. Secondly, the Protestant elite, deprived of its parliament, maintained a vice-like grip on local administration, the judiciary, the military and the professions — all of which were often heavily influenced by the anti-Catholic Orange Order. Thirdly, there was the continuing injustice of being force to pay tithes to the Protestant Church of Ireland. This encouraged violent attacks on individuals and property by agrarian secret societies — most notably the Ribbonmen.

Daniel O'Connell, a brilliant Catholic lawyer from an Old Irish gentry family in Co. Kerry, mobilized this Catholic discontent into a formidable political power. By means of a "Catholic rent" of a penny per month, large numbers of the lower classes became part of an organized political movement for the first time. The main objective of his Catholic Association, founded in 1823, was Catholic emancipation (ie. the right of Catholics to sit in Parliament and hold the highest offices of state), but it also set a pattern of lower-class political activity that was to prove highly influential. The Catholic Association's first major successes were the 1826 election victories for pro-emancipation candidates. In 1828, O'Connell himself stood for election in Clare. He wanted to bring matters to a head by forcing the government either to reject a duly-elected MP on the grounds of his religion, or to change the law to allow him to sit in parliament. His success was achieved by persuading the 40 shilling (£2) freeholders to ignore their landlord's directions. As voting was then an open, public affair (there were no secret ballots until 1874) the small freeholder had traditionally voted as his landlord directed, partly out of traditional deference to his social status and partly for fear of being evicted. O'Connell, with the aid of local parish priests, broke this bond and in so doing undermined aristocratic control of elected representatives.

Fearing serious unrest, the government of the Duke of Wellington, encouraged by Home Secretary Robert Peel, (both of whom had previously resisted emancipation) passed the Catholic Relief Bill which removed virtually all remaining restrictions on Catholics in Britain and Ireland — although to this day a Catholic cannot become the British monarch. Victory was achieved at a price, however. A bill to restrict the electorate by raising the property qualification in the counties from 40 shillings to £10 was passed simultaneously, thus destroying the very basis of electoral support which O'Connell had used to achieve emancipation.

Of more immediate importance to the disenfranchised 40 shilling freeholders, however, was competition for increasingly scarce land and the tithe issue. The former

was often a source of violent conflict between poor and middle-class Catholic farmers rather than Catholic farmer and Protestant landlord, but the latter brought rural Catholics into direct conflict with the state due to the Church of Ireland's position as a legally established pillar of Protestant society. The "Tithe War" which followed caused particularly violent clashes.

During the period in Ireland of Thomas Drummond, the Undersecretary from 1835 to 1840, education and public health were improved, and Catholics were appointed to top legal posts. In 1838 the Tithe Rent-charge Act reduced tithes by a quarter and swept away the confrontational means of collection by making landlords liable for their payment. Further reforms followed. The Irish Police was strengthened and made more impartial by banning members of the Orange Order (1836). The English Poor Law system was extended to Ireland — against the advice of those who knew the nature of Irish poverty — to provide workhouses run by elected boards of guardians (1838). In 1840 municipal government was reformed by abolishing the smaller town corporations and setting up elected bodies in the larger towns which were less susceptible to Protestant monopoly.

The return of a Tory administration in 1841 convinced O'Connell that further concessions were unlikely and, until his death in 1847, he threw his energies into a campaign for the repeal of the Act of Union. He founded the Repeal Association in 1840 in the hope of emulating his previous success with emancipation. Its campaign centered on enormous "Monster Meetings" at symbolic venues, such as the one at Tara (seat of the old high kings) on August 15, 1843. These meetings attracted hundreds of thousands and, as well as an expression of public will, they were an attempt to intimidate the British government without resorting to violence. However, O'Connell's veiled threats of popular unrest and his confident assertion that 1843 would be the "year of repeal" came to naught.

Unlike Catholic emancipation, there was very little British support for repeal of the Union. The government held firm and called O'Connell's bluff by banning the next "Monster Meeting" planned for Clontarf (the site of Brian Boru's defeat of the Vikings in 1014). O'Connell feared clashes with the military and ordered his supporters to abandon the meeting. This failure created tensions between O'Connell and activists of the recently-founded Young Ireland movement — an energetic group of romantic nationalists led by Thomas Davis, Charles Gavan Duffy and John Blake Dillon who hinted at violent revolution through their newspaper the *Nation*.

More pressing concerns now took precedence for most Irish men and women. As the momentum of the repeal movement faded, Ireland was overwhelmed by a tragedy of epic proportions which left its poor with little energy for political activism.

RIGHT: Faces of Ireland — our period starts with the depredations of the Great Famine and ends at a time of relative prosperity. In Connemara for much of the time farmers lived a harsh life with little involvement in the great political events going on around them. Here, a family in Sunday best in the 1920s.

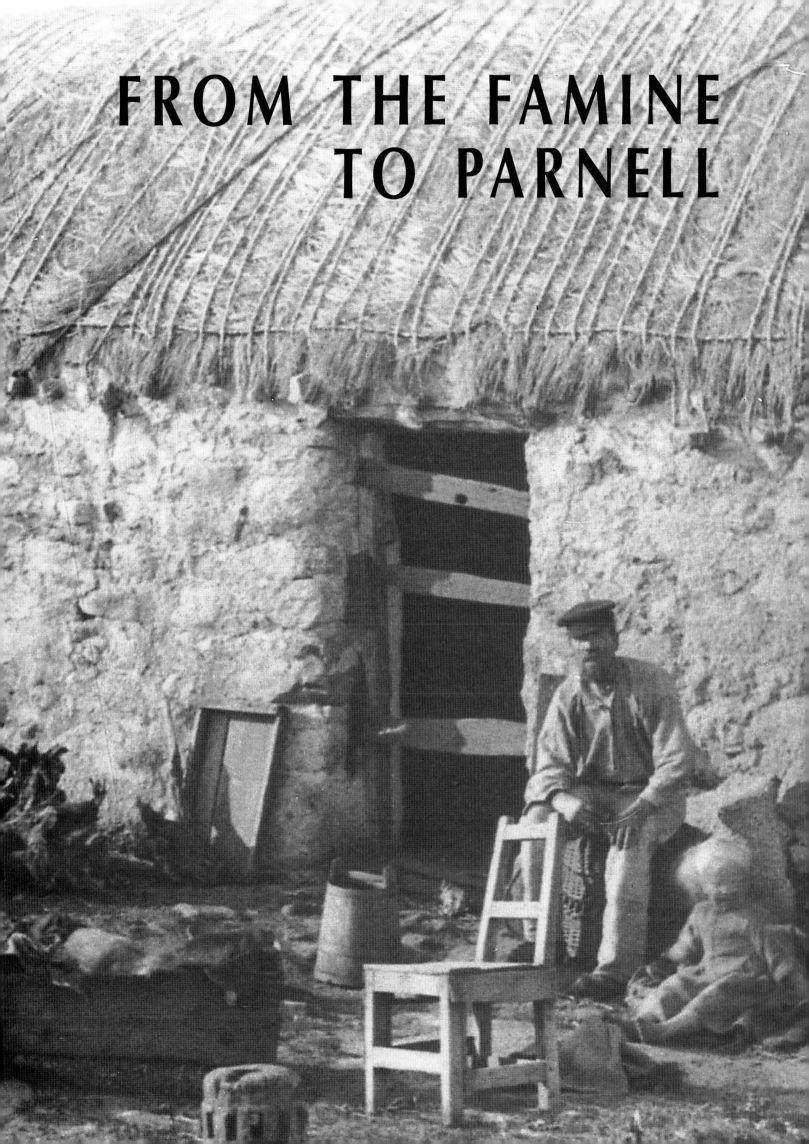

FROM THE FAMINE
TO PARNELL

ABOVE: King George IV lands at Howth near Dublin to pay a rare royal visit to Ireland in 1821.
No British monarch went to Ireland in the entire 18th century and the next visit would be Victoria's 79 years later.

PREVIOUS PAGE: An evicted family waits stoically outside their boarded up cottage with their few possessions.
Eviction rates generally decreased in the immediate post-famine years; they rose again during land agitation of the 1880s.

The great Irish famine was caused by a combination of three unhappy circumstances: the densely-populated character of rural Ireland, the dependence of much of that population on just one crop — the potato — and a devastating fungus called *Phytophtora infestans* which had been destroying potatoes all over the world since 1840. Hence the immediate cause of the famine was a natural one. But the full nature and extent of the famine cannot be separated from pre-existing economic relationships and political attitudes. To understand why the famine was so devastating and why the response of the British government so inadequate, we must look briefly at a number of wider issues, such as the place of Ireland within the Union, British attitudes towards Ireland, the economic theories of the day and the structure of Irish rural life.

Ireland is now a small country in terms of population, but relative to contemporary levels, this was less obvious on the eve of the famine. In 1841 Ireland contained over 8 million people out of a total UK population of around 26 million. In other words, nearly a third of the total population of the British Isles was Irish. (In contrast, by 1950 the population of the island of Ireland was less than 5 million out of a total British Isles population of well over 50 million — less than one tenth.) Thus in the mid-19th century, Ireland and Irishness were necessarily an important part of the British experience. Images of Irishness and direct experience of Irish people were very familiar to almost all Britons. Many Irish people lived and worked in Britain, and the British Army and Royal Navy were full of Irishmen. In the political sphere, the 105 Irish MPs at Westminster made up a significant portion of the House of Commons (about 15 percent) and could hold the balance of power between Whigs and Tories.

However, despite the important role of Ireland in the United Kingdom, in many respects its people were peripheral and different. Culturally, economically and religiously Ireland was sharply distinguished from Britain. Systems of land holding, the structure of the economy, work and social customs, and attitudes to law and authority all separated the two countries. Shortly before the famine, William Nassau, a respected professor of political economy at Cambridge University, observed:

"The people of England and of Ireland . . . are among the most dissimilar nations in Europe. One is chiefly Protestant, the other is chiefly Roman Catholic; one is principally manufacturing and commercial, the other almost wholly agricultural; one lives chiefly in towns, the other in the country. The population of one [England] is laborious but prodigal; no fatigue repels them — no amusement diverts them from the business of providing the means of subsistence . . . That of the other [Ireland] is indolent and idle, but parsimonious."

Despite his slightly condescending tone, Nassau was at

least sympathetic to the plight of the Irish poor. Many Britons, however, saw these "differences" in a less favorable light. The social and economic impact on Britain of Irish immigrants in search of work was profound, especially in the big cities such as Liverpool, Glasgow, Manchester and London. The Irish often provoked considerable hostility because of their readiness to accept undercut wages, and this led to the formation of Irish ghettos within British cities which reinforced negative images of difference.

The most important cause of hostility, however, was undoubtedly religion. Almost 80 percent of the Irish people were Catholics, but Catholics formed only a small minority in Protestant Britain, whose national self-image was largely founded upon the self-proclaimed virtues of Protestantism. Britons believed that from the Spanish Armada to the Napoleonic wars they had been forced against the odds to struggle for their survival against powerful Catholic countries such as France and Spain. Their Protestant religion was credited with uniting and inspiring the British people to remarkable achievements and, by 1850, these achievements were indeed remarkable. Britain had a huge empire and was the richest, most advanced nation on earth. Most Britons took for granted the idea that the immense wealth and power of such a relatively small country had to be due, at least in part, to God's approval of their Protestant faith. In their eyes God was an Englishman, which, of course, implied that he was also a Protestant. To be a Catholic, on the other hand, was at best to be deluded by superstition and idolatry and, at worst, to be excluded from God's chosen people. The practice of praying to the Virgin Mary and the saints for their intercession, and doctrines such as transubstantiation (by which the communion host and wine are believed to turn into the actual body and blood of Christ) were cited by Protestants as classic examples of the extreme irrationality of Catholicism.

Catholics, in the eyes of British Protestants, were also guilty of far more than mere idolatry and superstition. An outdated, 17th century, view of the nature of Catholic obedience to the pope left a constant shadow over the reliance of Catholic loyalty to the British state. How, many Britons asked, could Catholics obey the British crown and the Pope at the same time? Catholicism, therefore, was tantamount to treason in some Protestant eyes. For most Britons, Protestantism stood for vigor, virtue, rationality, loyalty, wealth and success, while Catholicism meant lethargy, vice, superstition, poverty, disloyalty and failure. Thus the British view that the Irish were lazy, feckless, ignorant and untrustworthy was intimately connected with religious differences.

These ideas of English superiority and Irish inferiority were reinforced by a connection with ethnicity. Such theories were completely spurious and utterly wrong. Both Britain and Ireland were ethnically very mixed and intermixed. Centuries of interbreeding between Celts, Romans, Anglo-Saxons, Scandinavians and Normans (to name only the most obvious ethnic groups) made a mockery of either Irish or English ethnic purity. The relative predominance of Celtic and Anglo-Saxon "blood"

ABOVE: A blight-affected potato preserved for posterity. The failure of the potato crop in four out of five years between 1845 and 1849 led to the worst catastrophe in Irish history.

undoubtedly differed in Ireland and Britain, but there were plenty of economic, historical and cultural factors to explain so-called differences in national character without resorting to crude notions of race.

Unfortunately, these deep-seated anti-Catholic and anti-Gaelic attitudes colored the views of many British observers and affected their reactions to Irish economic problems — problems which were essentially unconnected with religion or ethnicity. Either Irish poverty resulted from freely-taken moral and religious choices, which made it self-inflicted, or it was the result of ethnic inferiority, which meant that little could be done about it in any case. These views allowed many Britons to ignore Irish problems without too much guilt and conveniently omitted the role of British settlers and their governments in contributing to the conditions of Irish poverty. They concealed their ancestors' role in creating Ireland's problems behind a wall of prejudice, ignorance and superiority and allowed the government to wash their hands of Ireland without fear of too much public outcry. The combination of these views and the prevailing economic orthodoxy spelt disaster for Ireland.

By 1845, the doctrine of *laissez-faire* economics was dominant among the governing elite. The free market, with absolutely no checks or restraints, was seen as the ideal economic arrangement. In a perfectly free market,

the price of food (and there was food in Ireland, just not enough potatoes) is determined by what people are prepared to pay for it. The Irish peasant, if he had any money at all, could not hope to match the price that grain and other foodstuffs could get on the open market, and so he starved. To make matters worse, a respected political economist, Malthus, had predicted such events in overpopulated countries and could be cited to justify a hands-off approach. The Irish economy, so the argument ran, had surplus labor. Free Malthusian economics predicted starvation and emigration as the unfortunate but necessary means by which supply and demand came back into balance. Such attitudes seem callous today, but they are not that dissimilar to contemporary western responses to famine in the third world: in the 19th century, the country of Ireland seemed just as remote to many Britons, and its poverty seemed just as permanent and insoluble.

Even before the famine, when foreigners visited Ireland they were always shocked by its poverty. Whether rural or urban, Irish men and women were repeatedly declared to be among the most wretched in any part of Europe or the empire. Of course there were many rich and comfortable Irishmen. Parts of Dublin, after its extensive building projects of the 18th century, rivaled any city in classical elegance. In the north, Belfast had developed into a prosperous Victorian industrial city

with thriving linen, engineering and shipbuilding industries. The often fertile countryside provided a comfortable living for the larger farmer and the landed elite — even if many of the latter were heavily in debt. But poverty, squalor and economic insecurity were the lot of millions.

Commentators, both British and Irish, had struggled with the perennial problem of Irish poverty since the days of Swift and earlier. A wide variety of theories were put forward, but by the mid-19th century the most plausible focused on the many absentee landlords, the lack of investment in both agriculture and industry, and, most importantly, the difficulty of maintaining a dense and increasing rural population by the existing system of land-holding and agriculture.

The population of Ireland had increased rapidly in the late 18th and early 19th centuries and, although growth leveled out in the 1840s, had risen to 8.2 million. Ireland's population was high for its size and its relatively primitive agriculture. This population growth was accommodated uneasily by dividing the land into ever smaller and smaller holdings, and some pressure was relieved by substantial emigration even before the famine. But (with

ABOVE: Sir Robert Peel was the Tory prime minister at the time of the start of the famine and made a prompt response to the first signs of blight in September 1845, setting up a scientific commission to find the cause and buying maize from the US for famine relief.

the exception of the Belfast area) industrialization never took hold in Ireland. In Britain, the rural poor could migrate to the rapidly growing cities to find work: this was much more difficult to do in Ireland unless you wanted to emigrate. The shift from country to city in England meant that farms of over 30 acres were the norm; in Ireland farms under five acres were often the norm and those of the peasantry were much smaller. The lowest classes, especially in the west and south-west, survived by growing their own potatoes on patches of an acre or less, which they paid for in labor. This "conacre" system varied in detail across the country, but the tenants generally paid a relatively high rent for their little plot, which was often manured by the landlord and held from year to year with no security of tenure.

In those countries where grain was the staple food, such as England and America, plots of this size could never have supported a large family, but the potato is an incredibly efficient crop in terms of yield per acre. It is also very nutritious, and when supplemented with small quantities of protein in the form of buttermilk, bacon or herring, it provides a surprisingly well-balanced diet. Indeed, when there were enough potatoes, the Irish actually enjoyed a healthier diet than the peasantry in many other countries. Alongside the reports of Irish wretchedness, we find evidence that the Irish peasant was often

taller, heavier and stronger than his counterpart in Britain or on the Continent of Europe.

However, complete reliance on the potato crop had serious disadvantages. The vegetable was difficult to store, heavy to transport and it tended to rot after about 10 months. This meant short periods of dearth even in good years, and a complete inability to plan for bad ones. Hence, without prompt government action, even partial failure of the potato crop was bound to cause widespread malnutrition and starvation — as it had already done on many occasions before 1845. Total failure led to catastrophe. When the potato blight first took hold in 1845, at least two million peasants were already barely surviving at subsistence levels.

Given this scenario, the then Tory prime minister, Robert Peel, actually made a fairly enlightened and prompt response to the first signs of blight in September 1845. He set up a scientific commission to find the cause of the blight. He bought 100,000 tons of Indian corn (maize) from America to be sold at fixed, low prices from central distribution depots and set up a relief commission to oversee the distribution of this food. He ordered the

expansion of public works projects to provide employment. He repealed the protectionist Corn Laws, which lowered the price of wheat: but all these actions alone could not solve the problem. Lower bread prices helped, but as the worst affected had no money at all, it made little difference. Peel was not prepared to break the rigid laws of the free market, he did, however, bend them.

Peel's response was probably as rapid and humane as could be expected from most mid-19th century governments. The same cannot be said of the Whigs who came to power in the summer of 1846. The Whigs were firmly wedded to free market principles and had a tendency to regard most forms of relief as ineffective and a dangerous interference in the marketplace. In 1846, as the crisis deepened, the Whigs under the new prime minister, Lord Russell, decided against large-scale government intervention and thought the burden should rest primarily on Irish landlords. Thus the wholly inadequate system of famine relief often relied on private charity, local initiative and on whatever the Poor Law Unions could raise from rates levied on local landowners.

The government cut back — and then stopped completely — the public works' scheme, and then stopped importing maize in the hope that the new potato crop would be sound. When it became clear that it too was blighted, the government reluctantly and slowly began to provide relief once more. It was too little and too late for many in Ireland. From October 1846 onward people began dying from starvation in large numbers. A parish priest from Mayo, which was probably the worst affected county, observed:

"Deaths . . . innumerable from starvation are occurring every day; . . . the pampered officials . . . removed as they are from these scenes of heart-rending distress, can have no idea of them and don't appear to give themselves much trouble about them."

Public works eventually expanded to employ 728,000 by March 1847, but forcing starving, poorly-clothed men into hard physical labor in winter time was nothing less than barbaric. Eventually the government was forced to provide outdoor relief. The Soup Kitchen Act broke the free market taboo about giving away food, and the soup kitchens were feeding three million people by July 1847. Once again this was scaled back in the autumn as the new potato crop was sound, but it was inevitably very small due to the lack of seed potatoes to plant in the first place.

After 1847 the government advanced loans totaling £3 million to landlords to help them bear this cost, but the system failed miserably to provide enough food and shelter. Diseases such as typhus, relapsing fever, dysentery and cholera ravaged the country, and in remote areas with no access to workhouses, fever hospitals or soup kitchens, thousands simply died in ditches, on the roadside or in their cabins. The chief architect of this inhumane policy was Charles Edward Trevelyan, Assistant Secretary to the Treasury. Trevelyan feared that providing relief to what he saw as the naturally idle Irish poor would set a precedent and become a permanent burden on Britain. By 1847 he even thought that "too much had been done" arguing that from now on "Ireland must be left to the operation of natural causes" — by which he effectively meant that the government must let the Irish starve.

The Whig ruling elite in reality gave up on Ireland after this date, with the worst of the famine still to come. The potato crop failed again in 1848 and 1849, and yet no major new initiatives were taken. In May 1849 Lord Russell declared that it was not in the power of government to prevent the suffering and death in Ireland, but what he really meant was that he did not think the expense was justified. The British government acted shamefully, but many Irish landlords must also take some responsibility. There is plenty of evidence of good landlords who made considerable financial sacrifices to feed their tenants, but many did not provide food or employment on the scale that they could have. Evictions rose dramatically as many landlords tried to clear their land of starving tenants who had been unable to pay their rents since 1845 — there were nearly 20,000 evictions in 1850 alone.

Many landlords — from a mixture of motives — offered their tenants money to emigrate. Some acted with a degree of altruism in sending their tenants to America, Australia or Canada, but all knew the advantages of clearing their land of a troublesome and unproductive peasantry. Given the alternative of starvation, most peasants were happy to take up the offer. About a million emigrated during the famine, and by 1855 another million had followed them. The repeated failure of the potato crop between 1845 and 1849 also led to a million deaths from starvation and attendant disease.

The severity of the famine varied considerably from county to county and from parish to parish, often depending upon the goodwill and co-operation of local landlords

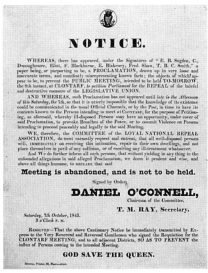

ABOVE: The episode of the cancelation of the "Monster Meeting" scheduled to take place at Clontarf on October 8, 1843, severely damaged O'Connell in the eyes of the Young Irelanders. (TOP) The government gives notice of a ban on the meeting. (CENTER) O'Connell cancels the meeting. Nevertheless the Repeal Association was still going in 1846 (ABOVE).

LEFT: An eviction in Co. Fermanagh (see caption on page 26).

and the availability of other foods. In general, the worst affected counties were Mayo, Sligo, Roscommon, Galway, Leitrim, Cavan and Clare — in other words, Connacht and some areas immediately adjoining it — whereas some counties in the north and east, such as Londonderry, Down, Louth, Dublin, Kildare, Wicklow, Carlow and Wexford, had much lower mortality rates. But all suffered great hardship: it was memory of this hardship and suffering, often transported across the North Atlantic to America, which would prove to be the most lasting legacy of the famine.

YOUNG IRELAND

For many Irishmen the terrible suffering of the famine only reinforced their desire for separation from Britain. This was especially true of Young Ireland founders Thomas Davis, Charles Gavan Duffy and John Blake Dillon. Young Ireland had been telling a potent and damning story of British involvement in Ireland in its weekly newspaper, the *Nation*, since 1842. Initially enthusiastic in its support of O'Connell's campaign for repeal of the Union, the Young Ireland movement soon took on a life of its own after the failure of O'Connell's constitutional methods to achieve repeal. As this new generation of activists sought new tactics, they began to clash with the aging and discredited Daniel O'Connell. They refused to rule out the use of force against Britain, and through the pages of the *Nation* they romanticized previous conflicts. The British were portrayed as an alien, conquering race, who should be ejected completely and immediately from Ireland.

When O'Connell categorically repudiated this approach in 1845, the repeal movement split between O'Connellite constitutional nationalists and the Young Irelanders who would not rule out force. This was a split which, in a variety of forms, would endure until independence and beyond. The ideology of Young Ireland differed from O'Connell's in a number of other areas in addition to the use of violence. Firstly, whereas O'Connell sought an independent parliament with Ireland maintaining some connection to Britain (probably through a joint

monarch), Young Ireland sought complete independence and the creation of a republic.

Secondly, Young Ireland sought to revive pride and interest in the Gaelic language and culture and considered O'Connell's attitude too English. Lastly, they differed from him over the role of religion. O'Connell was never openly anti-Protestant, but he appealed almost exclusively to Catholics. Young Ireland, while more anti-English than O'Connell, preached an Irish identity which could include all religions. Thus Young Ireland rhetoric, while very anti-English, was never anti-Protestant.

This last difference is hardly surprising, as many of Young Ireland's most influential leaders were themselves Protestant. Their unofficial leader until his death in 1845 was Thomas Davis, a Protestant of the Church of Ireland, and their most radical voice was John Mitchel, a Unitarian and the son of a Presbyterian minister. They both sought to fashion an Irish identity which could include all religions. This was laudable but inevitably problematic. While Davis and Mitchel condemned the Union, most Protestants had become increasingly attached to it. Despite the inclusiveness of Young Ireland rhetoric, therefore, most Irishmen associated Catholic resentment with opposition to the British connection.

This was an old problem for Irish patriots. Even in the optimistic early days of the French Revolution, the United Irishmen (whom Young Ireland consciously imitated) had faced huge difficulties uniting Protestant and Catholic in an inclusive national identity. The United Irishmen had some initial success, especially in bringing together Catholics and Protestant dissenters, but their rebellion of 1798 had ended in sectarian violence. Since their time, much had happened to further harden religious allegiances. O'Connell's use of priests to mobi-

ABOVE: Tenants on the Vandeleur estate in Kilrush, Co. Clare, being evicted during the Plan of Campaign in 1888. The Royal Irish Constabulary stands by to protect the landlords' agents while they batter down the the tenants' cottage wall to prevent reoccupation.

RIGHT: The Lord Lieutenant offers a £300 reward for the capture of Thomas Francis Meagher, John Blake Dillon and Michael Doheny for their part in the 1848 uprising. This was well over 10 years' wages for a common laborer!

lize Catholics for emancipation and repeal, the growth of the Orange Order, and the disproportionate affect on Catholics of the famine had all polarized attitudes to Britain around religious divisions.

By the time of the famine, repeal of the Union had become closely associated with a very Catholic brand of nationalism (although many Catholics supported a union of some sort), while the vast majority of Protestants wished to retain the Union. Despite these allegiances, Mitchel, in particular, was violent in his condemnation of Britain. By 1847 the most radical elements in Young Ireland were more convinced than ever that the British must be ejected from Ireland by force. Under the leadership of Mitchel and William Smith O'Brien they founded a revolutionary and republican movement called the Irish Confederation and began to prepare for rebellion.

In addition to a desire for separation, they drew on the economic ideas of James Fintan Lalor, who would prove one of the most influential theorists of Irish nationalism. Lalor, writing in the middle of the famine, recognized that Ireland faced serious economic problems beyond the famine which would not be solved by independence alone. The real issue, Lalor argued, was ownership of the land. His goal, therefore, was to sweep aside the discredited landlord system to create "a secure and independent agricultural peasantry." In a letter to Charles Gavan Duffy printed in the *Nation* he stated:

"I never will act with nor aid any organization limiting itself strictly to the sole object of dissolving the present connection with Britain and rigidly excluding every other. I will not be fettered and handcuffed. A mightier question is in the land — one beside which Repeal dwarfs down into a petty parish question."

In Lalor's view, every man's right to his share of the land was the "greatest of all our rights on this side of heaven — God's grant to Adam and his poor children for ever." But while a share in the land was a more fundamental right than national independence, the two were linked, as his most famous dictum made clear:

"The entire ownership of Ireland, moral and material, up to the sun, and down to the centre, is vested of right in the people of Ireland . . . they and none but they, are the land-owners and law makers of this island."

By the Lord Lieutenant General and General Governor of Ireland.

A PROCLAMATION.

CLARENDON.

WHEREAS We have received Information that *Thomas Francis Meagher, John B. Dillon, and Michael Doheny,* have been guilty of Treasonable Practices:

Now We, the Lord Lieutenant, being determined to bring the said *Thomas Francis Meagher, John B. Dillon, and Michael Doheny* to Justice, Do hereby offer a Reward of

THREE HUNDRED POUNDS

to any Person or Persons who shall secure and deliver up to safe custody the Person of any one of them, the said *Thomas Francis Meagher, John B. Dillon, and Michael Doheny;*

And We do hereby strictly charge and command all Justices of the Peace, Mayors, Sheriffs, Bailiffs, Constables, and all other Her Majesty's loyal Subjects, to use their utmost diligence in apprehending the said *Thomas Francis Meagher, John B. Dillon, and Michael Doheny.*

Given at Her Majesty's Castle of Dublin, this 28th Day of July, 1848.

By His Excellency's Command,
T. N. REDINGTON.

Printed by GEORGE and JOHN GRIERSON, Printers to the Queen's Most Excellent Majesty.

Most supporters of Young Ireland paid little attention to Lalor's explanation of Ireland's problems at the time, but he was a particular inspiration for Mitchel. Another was the revolutionary activity breaking out all over Europe in 1848, most notably in Paris where Louis Philippe was toppled in February, but also in the Austrian Empire, Germany and Italy. These events encouraged Mitchel in his plans for an Irish revolution. In February 1848 he broke away from the *Nation* to start his own more militant newspaper, the *United Irishman*. This portrayed Irish nationalist rebellion in almost spiritual terms and romanticized violent revolution and sacrifice for one's country. He rashly called for rebellion in the pages of the *United Irishman* and in May 1848 was arrested, along with other prominent Young Ireland leaders such as William Smith O'Brien and Thomas Meagher.

Mitchel was convicted under the new Treason-felony Act and transported to Tasmania for 14 years (he escaped in 1853). The other two were released, and a rebellion of sorts finally went ahead under the unlikely leadership of William Smith O'Brien. O'Brien represented all the untidy complexity of Irish history, for although he was the descendant of an old Gaelic family who could trace their ancestry back to Brian Boru, he was also a Protestant landowner and former MP. He had been educated at Harrow (one of the top English public schools) and had the accent and characteristics of an English gentleman. The rising he led on July 29, 1848, was not a serious challenge to the Union. Indeed, so minor was the clash with the Royal Irish Constabulary that it is some-

times disparagingly referred to as the Battle of Widow McCormack's Cabbage Patch, after the property in Ballingary, Co. Tipperary, which formed the centerpiece of the "uprising." O'Brien and Meagher surrendered and were convicted of high treason. They were given death sentences, later commuted to transportation for life. Charles Gavan Duffy claimed the rebellion "had not the slightest chance of success." The "sincere patriotism and courage" of Mitchel, he argued, were not matched by "practical capacity or the inestimable faculty of knowing what can be accomplished."

As Duffy also noted, a starving and submissive peasantry, conditioned by O'Connell to reject armed resistance, was hardly the stuff of successful revolution. But the real flaw in the romantic nationalism of Young Ireland was their attitude to the land issue. Middle-class intellectual idealists were unlikely to get the support they needed for a revolution without recognizing the basic needs and suffering of the people. Ireland faced serious economic problems which would not be solved by independence alone — as some farsighted individuals such as James Fintan Lalor recognized. The real issue for the people was ownership of the land. By yoking the question of land to the question of national independence, Lalor created a powerful connection that would provide the focus for much political activity between 1850 and 1900. But this connection was lacking for Young Ireland.

In short, the failure of these middle class revolutionaries was entirely predictable given the circumstances, and their actions were not widely supported at grass roots' level. But if their rebellion was ineffective, their ideology and their example proved quite the opposite, providing a powerful inspiration to all later nationalists from the Fenians to Patrick Pearse.

TENANT RIGHTS

A decade passed before the ideas of Young Ireland were taken up again by the Fenians in 1858, who, not surprisingly, were founded by remnants of the Young Ireland movement. Until this point, the 1850s were a confused and frustrating period for nationalist-minded Irishmen. There were a number of initiatives which seemed to hold promise, and which, in retrospect, foreshadowed future developments, but they ended in failure. The formation of local societies to protect tenants from eviction led to the Irish Tenant League in 1850. It had three main aims, often known as the "Three Fs": fair rents decided by independent evaluation, fixity of tenure and the freedom to sell their "interest" in the land to a new tenant (the so-called "Ulster custom").

The Tenant League was drawn together by Charles

Gavan Duffy, John Gray (editor of the *Freeman's Journal*) and Frederick Lucas (an English Catholic convert and editor of the *Tablet*). The league not only promised a degree of north-south co-operation, as local societies from Ulster and the south discussed the possibility of a nation-wide rent strike, it also contributed to the formation of an Irish parliamentary party at Westminster.

Between 1850 and 1852 both Whig and Tory governments had pursued highly anti-Catholic policies. In 1851 the Whigs denied Catholic bishops the right to use their full ecclesiastical titles, while a brief Tory government under Lord Derby in 1852 reinforced existing bans on Catholic processions. The passions stoked by these policies encouraged attacks on Catholic churches, and a Protestant mob attacked an illegal Catholic procession in Stockport in England. In response, the Catholic Defence Association was formed, and the 1852 elections saw victories for 40 Irish MPs associated with it. These MPs, who included Duffy and Lucas, pledged to pursue tenant rights (although not fixity of tenure), to oppose the Ecclesiastical Titles Act of 1851 and to maintain independent opposition to whichever British party, Whig or Tory, was in power.

This uneasy coalition soon faced serious difficulties. Support from Ulster drained away as soon as this "Irish Brigade" of MPs became heavily involved with Catholic issues. More damagingly, in December 1852 prominent MPs John Sadleir and William Keogh ignored their pledge and accepted jobs from a new Whig government. The party gradually dwindled over the next few years and after a further split in 1858 it died. A model of Irish MPs acting in concert to protect the rights of Irish farmers and Irish Catholics had been laid down, but its achievements were minimal. Charles Gavan Duffy, for one, was deeply disappointed. He gave up on Ireland as a lost cause and left for Australia in 1855, where he later became prime minister of the state of Victoria.

The tenant rights movement, which had been linked to the Independent Irish Party from the start, suffered in tandem. Many of its more comfortable members had little stomach for a national rent strike which might threaten their farms, and concerted action proved difficult. The movement was, anyway, of limited appeal: it had more to do with the temporary insecurity of grain farmers suffering from a fall in both the price and yield of their crop, than the poorest potato-dependent cottiers fighting eviction due to the famine. So when grain prices and crops improved after 1853, support was bound to diminish.

The issue of tenant rights was kept alive throughout the decade, however. In 1860, two acts were passed

which attempted, albeit unsuccessfully, to ease landlord-tenant relations. The Deasy Act tried to sweep away the last remnants of traditional and feudal land-holding by placing tenure on a purely contractual basis, but it had little effect, as most tenants had no contract. If anything, the act worked against the tenant, for it weakened his customary rights without putting him in a position of equal bargaining power when negotiating a new contract.

Another act did give tenants the right to compensation if they were evicted from land to which they had made their own improvements, but it was complicated and limited. In the final analysis, the Tenant Rights movement did little to solve the land question, but its achievement was not insignificant. It made a strong connection between land and politics which could be drawn on during the Land War of 1879–82.

FENIANISM

After the relative stagnation of the 1850s, in the next decade the nationalist sentiments aroused by Young Ireland were given a new outlet. In 1858 James Stephens and John O'Mahony, who had both been "out" with William Smith O'Brien in 1848, had set up the Fenian movement in Ireland and America. Having avoided arrest at Ballingary in 1848, Stephens and O'Mahony had fled to Paris, a hotbed of underground revolutionary activity following the aftermath of the revolutions of 1848. Their experiences in Paris convinced them that greater secrecy and more thorough organization would be needed if a future nationalist revolution was to have any chance of success. So in 1854 O'Mahony went to New York where, with the help of men like Michael Doheny, he began to organize financial and moral support from the ever-increasing Irish population in America.

O'Mahony was an intriguing character. Tall, vigorous and athletic, he was the charismatic man of action needed by any such revolutionary group. He was also a keen scholar of Gaelic culture, and the name Fenian was his doing. The ancient warrior elite of the Fionn cycle were known as Fianna: Fenian was invented by O'Mahony as a reference to them. He was not the most efficient organizer, nor the best judge of character, and often chose confidants, despite the reservations of his colleagues, who turned out to be informers. But without his energy and ability, the Fenians in America might never have got off the ground. He helped found in 1855 the Emmet Monument Association, whose name is a none-too-cryptic allusion to Robert Emmet's famous speech from the dock after his uprising in 1803. Emmet had asked that his epitaph be left unwritten until Ireland was a nation. The Emmet Monument Association was designed to bring this about and allow Emmet a proper memorial. By April

1859 the Emmet Monument Association had developed into the Fenian Brotherhood, which began to mobilize the potentially huge resources of Irish-Americans.

The activities of Stephens in Ireland also gave him a place in the pantheon of republican heroes. An engineer from Kilkenny, Stephens had been drawn into revolutionary nationalism through Young Ireland. His persistence in the cause through eight poverty-stricken years in exile in Paris was a vital link between Young Ireland and the Fenians. In 1856 Stephens finally returned to Ireland, where he undertook his famous walking tours all over the island to sound out republican and nationalist sentiment. In most areas he found little clearly articulated desire for independence, but he still sensed enough discontent to convince himself that a spirit of independence could be created and fostered.

Stephens was an excellent, if somewhat arrogant, organizer. He demanded absolute control of the organization he formed and was very thorough in the foundations he laid — rapidly incorporating local organizations of nationalist sentiment across the country under his leadership. The best-known of these was Jeremiah O'Donovan Rossa's Pheonix Society in Skibbereen, Co. Cork.

The Fenians wanted a democratic, independent republic, with votes for all adult males and the separation of church and state. They also sought reform of landownership and were scathing of aristocratic landlords, whether English or Irish. From 1859 they were rapidly

swearing in new members with the following secret oath:

"I, A.B., in the presence of Almighty God, do solemnly swear allegiance to the Irish Republic, now virtually established, and that I will do my utmost, at every risk, while life lasts, to defend its independence and integrity, and finally, that I will yield implicit obedience in all things, not contrary to the laws of God, to the commands of my superior officers. So help me God! Amen."

In keeping with its deliberately shadowy nature, there has always been some uncertainty over the origins of the name of the branch of the Fenians in Ireland. It was officially known as the Irish Republican Brotherhood (IRB) but was usually referred to simply as "the organization" or "the brotherhood" by its members. To the public at large, Fenian, the name of the more open American branch, did service for the whole phenomenon. The IRB's

LEFT: "Repeal of the Union!" O'Connell had died in 1847 but calls for the renegotiation of the Anglo-Irish connection continued, as this 1860 broadside from Cork attests.

BELOW: Fenian prisoners get their daily exercise in Mountjoy prison in Dublin. An attempt to free some of their comrades from Clerkenwell prison in London in 1867 killed a number of innocent local residents when a large gunpowder charge demolished a prison wall. This event shocked British public opinion and contributed to Gladstone's new policy of "justice for Ireland."

narrow economic interests of the class they had come from. Kickham went on to become head of the IRB after the Fenian uprising and achieved lasting fame through his popular nostalgic novel *Knocknagow*, published in 1873.

The Fenians' plans for a revolution were thwarted by the outbreak of the American Civil War in 1861 because they were dependent on funds, arms and men from America. While the war continued, revolution was impractical, and the movement concentrated on preparation and propaganda. The Fenians did pull off a major propaganda coup in 1861 when they brought back from America the body of Terence Bellew MacManus, a veteran of 1848, for a large-scale public funeral. He became one more in that long line of Irishmen who contributed most to Irish nationalism as a corpse.

The *Irish People* was founded in 1863 to preach revolution openly, a slightly bizarre enterprise for a supposedly secret society but a successful one in terms of generating support, for it coincided with the height of an agricultural depression. That the paper was allowed to continue for almost two years suggests a high degree of press freedom was maintained in mid-19th century Ireland — although it may also show that the Castle did not take Stephens and the IRB too seriously at this point.

One body which certainly did take the IRB seriously was the hierarchy of the Catholic Church. The role of the Catholic Church in politics moved markedly during the 1850s and 1860s away from popular involvement towards detachment and skepticism. Physical force nationalism was officially condemned — a position that would be maintained right through to independence. The dominant figure here was Cardinal Paul Cullen, Archbishop of Dublin, who modernized, centralized and Romanized the Irish Catholic Church with remarkable vigor and efficiency. He infuriated nationalists from Duffy to Davitt by his implacable opposition to clerical involvement in nationalist politics and his violent condemnation of Fenianism (he had, for example, tried to prevent the MacManus funeral in 1861). Duffy and Lucas blamed him for the break up of the Independent Irish Party, and the *Irish People* devoted much of its column space to counteracting his influence.

This is not to say that other clerics, including very senior ones such as Archbishop MacHale of Tuam, did not take a more active nationalist stand; but Cullen set the official tone that priests should concern themselves with the spiritual well-being of their parishioners, avoid contentious political subjects, and put the greater good of the church before political activity. In a broader sense, however, Cullen was highly political, for he had a vision of Irish society, and the church's role in it, which he was always willing to defend in the public arena. His encouragement of a huge program of church building created new focal points for "respectable" Catholic society.

Cullen also exerted himself on behalf of the poor in an age when poverty tended to be regarded as a self-inflicted social disease. He was especially active in promoting Catholic, as opposed to non-denominational, education — for example, in 1854 he had helped establish the ill-fated Catholic University of Ireland in Dublin. However,

rank and file members were usually Irish Catholics from the lower middle and working classes. In the towns, shopkeepers, artisans, schoolteachers and building workers were prominent, in the country small farmers and laborers were the norm.

IRB members were ordinary Irishmen, but they tended to be a step above those in genuine poverty: it was not generally a movement of the very poor. Largely due to the work of John Devoy, a significant number of members were Irishmen serving in the army — an ominous development for the government. These members were organized into cells. Nine privates reported to a sergeant. Nine sergeants reported to a captain. Nine captains reported to a "center." In an attempt to preserve secrecy, privates were not supposed to know the identities of any other members apart from those of their own cell.

The system did not work. The IRB was riddled with informers from very early on, and many of them at quite high levels. IRB leaders, like the leaders of Young Ireland, were usually well-educated and were often journalists. They were also sometimes Protestants, like Thomas Clarke Luby, who accompanied Stephens on his Irish walks. Luby later edited the main Fenian paper in Ireland (the *Irish People*) and was effectively Stephens' second-in-command. Other important members included Charles Kickham and John O'Leary. Both were the sons of shopkeepers and both proved important propagandists for the movement in the pages of the *Irish People* — often by criticizing the stifling effect on nationalist spirit of the he became increasingly out of touch with many in his flock over the national question — including many parish priests. In 1864, with some old O'Connellite politicians, he established an elitist and moderate National Association in an attempt to divert support from Fenianism. However, his goals of small-scale concessions to tenant rights, disestablishment of the Church of Ireland and improved Catholic education did little to fire the imagination of his fellow countrymen, and less to weaken the resolve of the Fenians.

The prospects for a Fenian rising suddenly appeared more favorable in 1865 when the American Civil War ended. Many thousands of Irish-Americans had fought on both sides in the conflict, and this large pool of military experience represented a vital resource for the Fenians — as well as a frightening development for the British government. Stephens promised a rising before 1865 was out and planned it for September 20, but the Castle got wind of it a few days beforehand and raided the office of the *Irish People* — arresting Luby, O'Leary and O'Donovan Rossa. Stephens was tracked down on November 11, but was rescued from Richmond prison in Dublin and escaped to New York via Paris (Fenian leaders were quite good at avoiding arrest and escaping from British jails and penal colonies). A young, but influential, activist, John Devoy, who had converted thousands of Irishmen serving in the army, called for an immediate rising; he was turned down by the Fenian council of war and was himself arrested in February 1866.

Without many of its leaders a rising would have been folly at that point, but most of the organization was still intact, and this organization was considerable. In 1865 Stephens had claimed, probably with considerable exaggeration, that 85,000 were sworn to the cause in Ireland. Stephens was more cautious after this point, however. The sobering experience of his arrest convinced him that the only realistic chance of success against British military might was in massive assistance — military and financial — from Irish-Americans. Despite the depth of anti-British feeling among Irish emigrants, and the obvious and increasing presence of American Civil War veterans in Ireland, this help had not been forthcoming in the scale needed. This fact led to disagreements between Stephens and O'Mahony in New York. As well as frustration at the meager funds that had been coming from American Fenians since 1858, their arguments had longstanding roots in O'Mahony's disapproval of the foundation of the *Irish People* and his removal of Stephens as "head center" of the worldwide organization in 1864. Stephens soon helped the "senate" wing of American Fenians (who wanted it governed collectively by a senate) to oust O'Mahony. Stephens himself became unpopular for refusing to go ahead with a rising in 1866 and was toppled from his position as head of the Fenian movement later that year.

By the time the rising came, most of the original leaders had either been arrested or deposed. The "acting chief executive of the Irish Republic" was now an American Civil War veteran, Colonel Kelly, who placed an experienced French soldier called Cluseret in command of mili-

IRISH WEEKLY INDEPENDENT. DECEMBER 2nd.

LARKIN · ALLEN · O'BRIEN

ATTACK ON THE POLICE VAN, SEPT 18TH 1867.

ABOVE: The "Manchester Martyrs" — Allen, Larkin, and O'Brien — were executed for their part in an attack on a police van in Manchester in 1867. The attempt to free Colonel Kelly went horribly wrong when a policeman in the van was shot and killed by an unknown Fenian who was probably trying to shoot the lock off the van door. The three "martyrs" were involved in the attack but almost certainly not the shooting incident. This commemoration dates from 1893 and aptly demonstrates the process of beatification which was the fate of many Irish nationalists.

LEFT: Cardinal Paul Cullen was the most influential 19th century Irish cleric. He reorganized and modernized the Catholic Church and took a hard line against Fenian activity.

tary affairs. Once again the government knew the rising was coming. On February 11 the Fenians were forced to call off a daring arms raid on Chester Castle in north-west England at the last minute. When the poorly-organized rising finally came on March 5, 1867, it was a complete failure.

The Fenians' plans were betrayed by an informer, which led to the capture of a senior commander, Massey, on a railway platform in Limerick on March 4. Massey immediately revealed his knowledge of the plans for the rising, and Cluseret, hearing of his arrest, fled to France. A number of local uprisings went ahead anyway, and a few police barracks were captured in counties Cork and Dublin, but they were a futile gesture with no hope of ultimate success. The most lasting benefit to the nationalist cause came, not unusually, from the anger aroused among Irishmen by the heavy-handed approach of the British government in the aftermath of the rising.

In September, Colonel Kelly and another Fenian active in the rising, Captain Deasy, were arrested in Manchester. A successful attempt to rescue them from a prison van led to the shooting, probably accidentally, of police Sergeant Brett when an unidentified Fenian tried to shoot the lock off the van door. Three Fenians who had been present but who had not fired the shot were tried and executed for murder. Their sentence was received with outrage in Ireland, and Allen, Larkin and O'Brien immediately became known as the "Manchester Martyrs." It takes two to make a martyr and the British played their part to perfection.

Adept at making the most of such events, the Fenians

ABOVE: Isaac Butt, the founder of the Irish Parliamentary Party, caricatured in Vanity Fair *in 1873. Butt, a Protestant, started his political career as an independent-minded Tory unionist before his conversion to Home Rule.*

achieved more with the reaction to these executions than they ever could have hoped to from their poorly-planned rising. The propaganda value was immense and the executions were long remembered as an infamous case of British injustice.

THE ORIGINS OF HOME RULE

The epilogue to the Fenian rising was a bomb blast at Clerkenwell Prison in London. This attempt to rescue captured Fenians was probably the most effective act of the whole campaign, for in killing a number of innocent civilians who just happened to live by the prison, it caused such an outrage in Britain that it finally brought home the Irish question to senior politicians in a manner they could not ignore. Gladstone, the Liberal leader then in opposition, determined to seek solutions to Irish problems with greater urgency. When Gladstone's Liberals were elected in 1868, they quickly brought in two measures which signaled the intention to do "justice to Ireland."

First, in 1869, parliament passed the Irish Church Act to disestablish the Church of Ireland. The act ended the privileged legal position the church had enjoyed since the 16th century and placed it on the same footing as any other church in Ireland. The settlement, in terms of the land and buildings it allowed the church keep, was financially generous considering it had the allegiance of less than 15 percent of the population, but it sent a powerful

signal to Irish Protestants that British politicians, and especially Gladstone, would not automatically defend their interests if these got in the way of the greater public good. The second measure, the Land Act of 1870, sent equally powerful signals to Irish landlords, although as we shall see later, it was largely ineffective.

Gladstone was not the only mainstream politician to be deeply affected by Fenianism; Isaac Butt was another. One of the leading lawyers in Ireland, Butt was a Tory, a Protestant and in his youth had been a Unionist. However, the behavior of the British Government during the famine, as well as the spirited behavior of Young Ireland and the Fenians (some of whom he defended in court), convinced him that Ireland should govern more of her own affairs. In 1870, he founded the Home Government Association, which eventually gave rise to an independent Irish Home Rule party in parliament.

Butt was no radical. Indeed, the origins of the Home Government Association owed much to Protestant dismay at the way their church could be disestablished so easily from Westminster. The majority of the original members were wealthy Protestants and a high proportion of Conservatives (although many Catholics, Liberals and even a few Fenians also joined). His goal was a respectable Irish parliament based on the British model of Commons and Lords, containing Tory and Liberal, Catholic and Protestant. Imperial and defence matters would still be the preserve of Westminster and the monarch of Britain would still be the monarch of Ireland, but all domestic affairs and most taxation would be overseen from Dublin, rather than London.

In 1874, the first general election with secret ballots took place, which meant that electors could vote free from the scrutiny of their landlords or employers. The result was a resounding success for the Home Rulers — who were now organized as the Home Rule League — with 59 MPs. Apart from the brief experiment with an Irish party in the 1850s, Irish party politics tended to follow the British pattern of Liberal/Whig or Conservative. This result broke that trend. The Conservatives were still well represented with 33 seats and many Home Rulers were really old Liberals of questionable commitment to the cause; nevertheless a new pattern of Irish party politics had been set.

The new grouping was not yet an organized political party in the modern sense. There was no formal program or manifesto, and its MPs pursued a variety of different goals (such as amnesty for imprisoned Fenians, a Catholic University and land reform), which tended to reduce their effectiveness on the pursuit of Home Rule. However, the party was the embryo of a highly effective political force. Butt became a respected and articulate advocate of Irish self-government at Westminster, but he failed to convince either of the main British parties of the merits of Home Rule. Disraeli's Conservative government (1874–80) was never very interested in Ireland to begin with, and important world crises in the Balkans and Africa gave the Tories all the excuses they needed to ignore it. When this fact became increasingly clear to other Home Rule MPs, a number of more radical, and less urbane, members began to disrupt the business of the House of Commons with interminable speeches. By bringing British law-making to a standstill, this obstruction was a highly effective way of focusing the attention of British MPs on Ireland.

The Belfast MP and Fenian Joseph Biggar originated the policy, and his success soon attracted other Irish MPs, including another Fenian — John O'Connor Power — and a young Protestant landlord from Wicklow called Charles Stewart Parnell. Butt was appalled by this tactic, but financial difficulties forced his absence from parliament for long periods and he gradually lost his grip (never very strong to begin with) on the party. As Butt's influence waned during 1877 and 1878, a number of younger Home Rulers jostled for leadership. The eventual victor was Charles Stewart Parnell, but this had by no means been a foregone conclusion. A poor public speaker, his passionate nature and undoubted abilities were often hidden beneath a stiff, cold and reserved manner.

John O'Connor Power and Frank Hugh O'Donnell were seen by many as more attractive leaders until 1879, but Parnell, despite his inexperience, rapidly developed into a masterful politician. He acquired an unerring sense of what could and could not be achieved. He knew when to lead public opinion and when to follow. Furthermore he was skilled at using (one could almost say hijacking) other movements when their goals matched his own. He flirted with the Fenians and showed sympathy with their aims — which helped establish his nationalist credentials — but he never joined them or became a prisoner of their goals. He also inherited, partly through his American mother, a deep dislike of the English and detested the way many of them looked down upon his countrymen. In 1877 Parnell had become president of the British branch of the Home Rule Confederation after a split with Butt, and with Butt's death in May 1879 Parnell was best placed to assume his leadership of the Home Rule Party itself.

The event which helped Parnell become leader was the Land War. As shall be explained, the instigation of the Land War was far from Parnell's doing, but his handling of it established his authority in the Home Rule Party and in Ireland generally. He surfed a tidal wave of popular unrest with great skill — balancing a number of different interests and choosing the right moment to jump off.

THE ECONOMY AFTER THE FAMINE

Between the famine and the Land War of 1879–82, there were considerable changes in the economic and social structures of rural Ireland, especially in the immediate post-famine years. In addition to the massive drop in population caused by wholesale starvation and emigration, about one in ten landlords had gone bankrupt because of the famine. As a result, the next five years saw around 15 percent of the land change hands. This process was aided considerably by the Encumbered Estates Acts of 1848 and

RIGHT: Charles Stewart Parnell succeeded Butt as leader of the Home Rule Party after the latter's death in 1879. He rose to eminence on the back of the Land War and proceeded to dominate Irish politics until his fall from grace in 1890.

1849, which helped the most indebted landlords to sell their land. The government's hopes for an influx of new "improving" landlords from Britain was disappointed, however, as almost all the new landlords were Irish, and many were simply speculators attracted by cheap land.

In the immediate aftermath of the famine many landlords, old and new, evicted the poorest and smallest tenants, and some even increased rents to force remaining tenants out. Severe rent rises, however, were unusual and annual evictions decreased rapidly from a high of 19,949 in 1850 to 2,156 by 1854. This process helped landowners and the more prosperous tenant farmers to consolidate their holdings and to increase the average size of Irish farms. The long term result of these changes in population and ownership was that, except in parts of the west, the number of small cottiers subsisting on less than five acres decreased dramatically. Whereas 45 percent of all farms had been less than five acres in 1841, by 1881 this figure was only 13 percent.

Emigration continued to ease pressure on the land as the population decreased from 6,552,385 in 1851 to 5,174,836 in 1881. Those cottiers who did not emigrate often became landless laborers while "strong farmers" — with farms of 15 to 30 acres or more — became increasingly common. This depopulation and structural change allowed a shift to pasture from tillage, as cattle, pigs, and sheep became more profitable than wheat. There was still great poverty, however, especially in the west, but in the 25 years following the famine rural Ireland did see increased living standards. The strong farmer class in particular became more prosperous as the century progressed. From 1850 the prices they received for their produce increased at roughly double the rate of their rents — and more for livestock.

However, these positive changes occurred alongside growing tensions. Farmers' tenures were often insecure. For example, in 1871 over 75 percent of tenant farmers held their land at will (under no legal contract). Thus, in acute periods of depression, such as 1860–64 and most notably 1879–83, many farmers were vulnerable to eviction. Between 1856 and 1878 annual rates of eviction were actually quite low — usually less than 1,000 a year (fewer than 1.5 per thousand properties). Hence in this period the traditional picture of landlords extorting high rents or evicting their tenants is not typical (although it certainly occurred). Absentee landlords were also less common than popular myth might suggest, and the amount of rent leaving the country decreased significantly after the famine, for the land that changed hands went primarily to Irishmen. By 1871, less than a quarter of Irish land was owned by landlords living in England and the rent they took was less than that paid to landlords resident in Dublin.

This level of absenteeism is still significant, but it suggests that the received images of Irish landlords as being wholesale rack-renters, evicting tenants at will and enjoying their rents as absentees, should be treated with some skepticism. One thing that can be said about landlords as a whole is that they jealously guarded the rights of private property. The solution of Ireland's agricultural problems obviously required radical improvements in security of tenure and rent control, but this was always going to face severe opposition from powerful landed interests in parliament. It would inevitably involve desecrating the sanctity of private property, and this had far-reaching implications for English landowners as well as Irish (who, of course, were often the same individuals). Thus Gladstone's first attempt to tackle the issue (the Land Act of 1870) had its provisions for tenant rights so watered down in parliament that it had little real effect, and one of the most important demands of farmers — rent control — was rejected as an interference with "the just rights of property." However, the act did increase the compensation available to tenants for their improvements and gave legal recognition to customary rights — which reversed the ethos imposed in the 1860 Deasy Act. Along with similar clauses in the Irish Church Act of 1869, it also set an important, if ineffective, precedent by providing government loans for tenants who wished to buy their lands. A deposit of one-third was required, which was far too much for most, but the scheme sent a clear message to the landlord class that ownership of the land by its occupiers was seen by many Liberals and nationalists as the long-term solution to the land question.

Ireland also faced serious economic problems in the cities as well as on the land. In much of the rest of Europe, and especially in Britain, urbanization and industrialization provided an outlet for farmers and peasants pushed off the land. This was not the case in Ireland; industry was underdeveloped throughout this period and the country remained fundamentally agricultural. The major exception to this rule was Ulster, which contained the only heavily industrialized area in Ireland (around Belfast and the Lagan valley). Belfast's wealth was based initially on the linen industry, but engineering and shipbuilding soon developed.

By the second half of the 19th century Belfast had as much in common with the industrial cities of northern England and Scotland as it did with the rest of Ireland. Not surprisingly, this heavily Protestant area rapidly developed a very different political and economic outlook to the rest of Ireland. Economically, the British connection was vital to its well-being, and this reinforced its increasingly strident Protestantism and Unionism. Thus the one major Irish industrial city was not an attractive option for internal migration for most Catholic Irishmen, especially as Catholics were severely discriminated against in its factories and shipyards.

Young men and women coming of age in the 1870s, therefore, faced difficult decisions. The availability of land had diminished rapidly after the immediate post-famine years as farmers became determined to consoli-

RIGHT: The well-dressed men and women strolling down Belfast's Castle Place are an indication of the wealth and confidence of Ireland's only late-19th century industrial city.

date their farms and pass them on to a single son. There were few big cities within Ireland with jobs enough for mass migration. The only option was often emigration to jobs in foreign cities — but when widespread economic depression in America and Britain ruled this out, and agricultural depression in Ireland affected work on the land, Ireland's precarious economic system began to break down.

THE LAND WAR 1879–82

Irish economic problems came to a head around 1879, when an agricultural depression coincided with more repeated failures of the potato crop. This resulted in great hardship and insecurity, especially in the west where the potato crop was poor for a disastrous third year running. Even in the more prosperous areas, Irish farmers could not compete with the flood of cheap American wheat coming onto the market. The threat of another serious famine loomed. The trend of low levels of evictions since the mid-1850s quickly reversed as an average of 3,000 families per year were turned out of their homes in the period 1879–83. Agrarian outrages rocketed, from 301 in 1878 to a peak of 4,439 in 1882 — which amounted to well over half of all reported crimes in Ireland.

As with the famine, the worst-affected areas were in the west, with Mayo at the epicenter. The deeply-held nationalist feelings of Mayo had been revealed by the election of John O'Connor Power, a Fenian, as one of their MPs in 1874. This republican sentiment now combined with growing hardship to inspire local political activity on an impressive scale. Activists such as James Daly, editor of the *Connacht Telegraph*, and Matt Harris, the election agent of O'Connor Power, helped in the formation of tenant protection societies, but this was ultimately a grass roots' movement whose energy came from the small and medium size farmers themselves.

On August 16, 1879, the Land League of Mayo was founded by Michael Davitt, and by October 21 a National Land League, with Parnell as president, was founded in Dublin. Having Parnell at the head of the Land League contributed enormously to its success, but the real orchestrator was Michael Davitt, one of the key figures in late 19th century Ireland. Born in Mayo in 1846, Davitt had spent much of his life in the English mill town of Haslingden in Lancashire after eviction had forced his family to emigrate in 1851. He worked long hours in the mill as a child until he lost an arm in the machinery when he was 11 years old. His injury forced him to leave the mill and changed the course of his life. Through studying with the local postmaster he gained an education he would never have otherwise had, and in 1865 he joined the Fenians. In 1870 he was jailed for 15 years for his involvement with the IRB but was released

Right: A forest of masts at the mouth of the Lagan in Belfast harbor. Despite its smaller size, Belfast's growing industrial base meant that it replaced Dublin as Ireland's largest port by the end of the 19th century.

William Gladstone was a colossus of British politics from the 1860s until his death in 1894. Much of his career was dogged by Irish issues. These two Weekly Freeman *cartoons from 1881 show the dilemmas he faced during the Land War. The first (ABOVE) shows him carrying two seemingly contradictory remedies — a favorable Land Bill and Coercion — while "Mrs Erin" defiantly stamps on landlordism and rejects his half measures. The second (BELOW) shows a popular British view that the Land League was actually doing the coercing — its threats of violence forcing Gladstone into a Land Act widely perceived as an illegitimate attack on property.*

in 1877, whereupon he immediately threw himself into political activity. He worked with John Devoy in America to persuaded Fenians (now organized as Clan na Gael) to combine support for independence with support for land reform.

This "new departure" of American and Irish Fenians was an important development which allowed co-operation with constitutional nationalists. While it was condemned by Kickham and the hard-line Supreme Council of the IRB in Paris, many Fenian and IRB men ignored their concern that the revolutionary spirit would be contaminated by co-operation with moderate nationalists for useful reform. Support for the Land League and Parnell may have been a means to an end for many hard-line nationalists, but their energy and commitment was vital.

On his return from America, Davitt was appalled by conditions in his native Mayo. The potato crop of 1879 was only one quarter of that of 1876 — and this followed on from two partial failures in 1877 and 1878. Davitt rapidly established himself as chief organizer of the growing agitation over the agricultural crisis and, with the help of Devoy, persuaded Parnell to lend his support. As tensions rose, a series of large meetings in Irishtown, Milltown and Westport galvanized the resistance of small farmers to high rents and eviction. At the Westport meeting of June 1879, Parnell advised these farmers "to hold a firm grip of your homesteads and lands."

"You must not," he argued, "allow yourselves to be dispossessed as your fathers were dispossessed in 1847." Grievances with English and Irish landlords, whether justified or not, were real in the popular consciousness, and many small farmers required little persuasion to take his advice to heart.

The huge strength of support for the Land League came from a wide geographical and social base, which reflects the fact that the struggle was really quite different across the country. In the wealthier east, prosperous farmers facing low crop prices wished to strengthen

A Land Act, which met some of tenants' demands for security of tenure and rents fixed by tribunals, had been passed in August, but the Land League was unhappy with it and tried to obstruct its operation. The government's reply was swift. When it arrested Parnell and other Land League leaders on October 13, 1881, the league started a "No Rent" campaign in response (ABOVE). A week after the arrests the government suppressed the Land League itself by proclaiming it an illegal organization (BELOW).

their long-term position with respect to the landlord and used the league simply to avoid paying rent until the last possible moment. In the poorer parts of the west, still dependent on the potato, it was literally a struggle for survival. Support from laborers, both rural and urban, was often lukewarm, as they had no land to hold on to.

However, apart from the landlords themselves, the league successfully allied an impressive and diverse array of interests. Local priests invariably threw their weight behind the league, even if their hierarchy was more cautious. Moderate Irish MPs, who were dismayed by the violence, nevertheless recognized the suffering of small farmers and the justice of their case. Huge sums of money flowed in from America to fund the league (Davitt estimated it at $250,000), and massive amounts of private charity from Ireland, America and Britain ensured that the dreadful famine was not repeated — which in itself testifies to a shift in popular opinion on Irish economic problems.

Parnell fought the general election of 1880 on the land issue and off the back of an immensely popular American tour. His own election for three different seats demonstrated the widespread support for him and the Land League. Less than half of the 59 Home Rule Party candidates elected to Westminster were committed supporters of Parnell at this stage, but he was obviously the rising star. Using his leadership of the league, with all the popular power that implied, he was able to enhance his importance in parliament. By May 1880 he was made chairman of the Irish Parliamentary Party: a position from which he dominated the next decade of Irish history. The Land League itself did not openly encourage violent activity, it was a perfectly legal organization, and much of its activity was charitable. One of its main functions, for example, was to provide evicted families with shelter and food.

The league was full of ex-Fenians at all levels and did provide moral support for agrarian violence and intimidation. This was

ABOVE: *Captain Boycott gave a new word to the English language. The moral and commercial isolation in which Lord Erne's land agent was placed during the Land War eventually forced him to leave for England in an ambulance cart protected by cavalrymen.*

BELOW: *Lease-burning was a common feature of the Land War. This scene in Kildare is typical of the mass meetings that were to lead to the accusation that the leaders of the Land League were inciting unrest in the country.*

considerable on both sides. Landlords and their agents were threatened, attacked and (as in the case of Lord Mountmorres) murdered. Their animals were brutally maimed and large-scale physical damage was inflicted on their crops and property. The league's formal role was to organize popular demonstrations against evictions by landlords and to ensure that these landlords, along with any farmers brave enough to move onto land cleared by eviction, were shunned by the rest of the community. This tactic of complete social and commercial non-cooperation was so successful it gave the English language a new word — "Boycott," after the treatment meted out to Lord Erne's agent, Capt. Charles Boycott of Co. Mayo.

The Gladstone government reacted with measures designed to stamp out the violence: troops were routinely used. In February 1881 Davitt was arrested, and in March the government passed two acts — the Protection of Person and Property Act and the Peace Preservation Act.

These gave additional powers to the police and army, set up special courts without juries to convict agitators, and suspended the right of Habeas Corpus — which normally prevents arrest without charges being laid for a specific crime. However, Gladstone's response also contained important concessions. His Land Act of August 22, 1881, finally secured the principle of the "Three Fs." It set up land courts to fix fair rents, protected tenants from eviction provided they paid their rent, and allowed tenants to sell their interest in the land, as well as the improvements made, to an incoming tenant. This was a radical measure by the standards of the day and was seen by English and Irish landlords as a violation of the rights of property.

The Land Act had serious flaws; it did little for the poorest farmers in the west and ignored farmers in arrears with their rent — precisely the people who needed the most protection. Parnell knew it would not satisfy radicals in the Land League, but he also knew it was a major concession. So he helped get the bill through parliament and then criticized it violently to retain the support of the hard-liners. Gladstone was exasperated by Parnell's obstruction of the new Land Act. He responded in October by outlawing the Land League and imprisoning Parnell and its other leaders on a charge of conspiring to prevent rent payments. As a result, the violence actually increased, and Gladstone was forced to negotiate with Parnell to prevent chaos in the countryside.

The beginning of the end of the Land War came in May 1882 with the "Kilmainham Treaty." Gladstone agreed to release Parnell and other Land League leaders from Kilmainham jail and to rectify the problems in the Land Act, in return for their assurance that they would disown the violence and bring the Land War to an end.

Some more militant activists, including in their number Davitt, wanted to continue the war with national rent strikes. Their ultimate goal of nationalized land ownership, however, was out of step with the aims of the small farmer, who simply wanted to own the land himself or, failing that, to pay a low rent with a secure tenure. The Land War was ultimately a conflict for control of land waged by tenant farmers for economic security, rather than a quasi-nationalist uprising.

Judged by these standards, the tenant farmers won: the 1881 Land Act was a pivotal event in the transformation of Irish agriculture. Tenant farmers had established their right to a secure stake in the land they worked, and the shift from landlordism to widespread occupier ownership of small and medium-size farms was clearly signaled. This process would not be fully realized until the early 20th century, however, when the effect of legislation to allow tenants to buy their land using government loans eventually kicked in. Ironically, despite all of Gladstone's efforts, it was not the Liberals but the Tories who really "solved" the land question. The Ashbourne Act of 1885 allowed tenants to borrow the entire amount needed to buy their farms, to be paid back over 49 years at 4 percent interest. Successive acts, culminating in the Wyndham Land Act of 1903, gave even easier terms of repayment.

The final nail had been hammered into the coffin of

ABOVE: "Cause and effect . . ." a cartoon from **Weekly Freeman** *of April 1, 1882. A Land Leaguer is manhandled by a policemen while a masked gunman looms in the background. The Land Leaguer is saying: "If you had let me expose my grievances on a public platform in broad daylight, he would not be standing behind me."*

LEFT: "Buckshot" Forster, Chief Secretary for Ireland, vehemently advocated the arrest of Land Leaguers and subsequently resigned when the leaders were released from jail in May 1882 under the Kilmainham Treaty.

ABOVE: Recreation time in Kilmainham Gaol. Parnell, Davitt and other leaders of the Land League were imprisoned in October 1881. As this sketch shows, they were afforded privileges not accorded to other prisoners.

RIGHT: Portrait of Parnell.

old-style Irish landlordism. Before the Land War nearly 70 percent of the land was rented; by the outbreak of World War I two-thirds was owned by the people who actually farmed it.

PARNELLISM

There was one final act of violence during the era of the Land War — albeit largely unconnected with that struggle — which left a mark on Anglo-Irish politics. Earlier, during the late 1870s, many Fenians adopted a new policy or "new direction" of co-operation with constitutional nationalists. Their tradition had not died out completely, it had merely gone underground. After the Kilmainham treaty, the chief secretary, Forster, had resigned in protest. Lord Frederick Cavendish, who arrived to take his place, was generally seen as an appeasement figure who would usher in a more conciliatory era. But on the day of his arrival he was stabbed to death in Pheonix Park along with his undersecretary, Thomas Burke (an Irish Catholic), by a little known group called the Invincibles. Public opinion in both countries was horrified and, in a knee-jerk reaction, a Crime Prevention Act was passed by the Government.

The incident did not materially affect either the final settlement of the Land War, or Gladstone's attitude to Parnell, but it would come back to haunt the latter. After his release from prison, Parnell set about steering the political machinery of the Land League towards Home Rule. The Land League was replaced by the Irish National League, comprizing much the same support but more firmly under the control of the Irish Parliamentary Party. By 1884 Parnell had won the support of the Catholic Church by agreeing to push for separate Catholic education, and the strength of support for Parnell began to convince Gladstone that Ireland must have a measure of Home Rule.

Gladstone's reasons for converting to a belief in home rule were a mixture of principle and pragmatism. Irish issues were bound to be a continuing source of division, obstruction and aggravation within British politics if left unresolved — but he undoubtedly had a genuine desire to improve the prosperity of Ireland as well as the way it was governed. He had supported the right to self-government in other countries and thought that government unaided by the people was unlikely ever to be successful in the long term. After the general election of December 1885, in which the Irish Parliamentary Party won 86 seats, it had become clear that the Conservatives could cancel out the Liberal majority with the support of Home Rule MPs. This must have had weight in Gladstone's calculations, but it had also become clear that most Irishmen did not endorse the present system of government. Only in eastern Ulster and the University of Dublin were Unionist MPs returned.

So in 1886 Gladstone brought his first Home Rule Bill before parliament. The influential radical Joseph Chamberlain, leader of an important wing of the Liberal party, immediately opposed Home Rule as an assault on the integrity of the United Kingdom and the British Empire — even though he had proposed his own limited version only a few months earlier. The Conservatives (always more pro-Union) naturally opposed the measure, and all the old stereotypes of Irish character resurfaced to support the case that the Irish were incapable of governing themselves. The Home Rule Bill failed and split the Liberals, bringing down the government. Indeed, so damaging were the divisions created by the bill (with a group of Liberal Unionists under Chamberlain defecting to the Tories) that for the next 20 years the Liberals could only regain power for one brief period between 1892 and 1895.

Nevertheless, progress had been made. For the first

ABOVE: *Lord Frederick Cavendish, who was appointed Chief Secretary for Ireland following Forster's resignation.*

BELOW: *The Invincibles had been planning to kill Forster for some time but changed their target to Cavendish after Forster's sudden departure. Carey, an Invincible not involved in the Phoenix Park murders, turned state's evidence against his fellow-conspirators. He would be killed as an informer as he left by boat for Africa and a new life.*

RIGHT: *The murders as illustrated in* Le Monde *of May 1882.*

time since the Union, a major British political party had adopted Home Rule, and at the end of the decade, the prospects for a successful Home Rule Bill still looked good should a new Liberal government get in. The reputation of Parnell stood at an all-time high after his vindication from the *Times'* accusation that he was implicated in the Phoenix Park murders of 1882. The *Times'* shoddy campaign to implicate Parnell relied on a series of letters which supposedly expressed Parnell's regret at having to condemn the murders in public — the inference being that in private he approved of them. When they were shown in early 1889 to be the forgeries of a Dublin journalist called Richard Pigott, Parnell was praised in English liberal circles as the honorable victim of a disgraceful plot to blacken his name. Unfortunately for the cause of Home Rule, Parnell's enhanced reputation did not last long. His long-standing affair with Katherine O'Shea, wife of fellow Irish MP Captain William O'Shea, was made public knowledge when Captain O'Shea filed for divorce naming Parnell as co-respondent (in other words his wife's lover).

William O'Shea had probably known of the affair since the early 1880s. He went along with it to further his political career and to safeguard the money he received from Katherine's aunt. With the death of the aunt William O'Shea did not receive the money he had hoped for from Katherine's inheritance and began divorce proceedings, probably in an attempt to blackmail her. Parnell was deeply in love with Katherine and welcomed the divorce as an opportunity to marry her. They had been living together for years (he called her his "wifie") and she had borne him at least two, possibly three, children. As the full details of their relationship came out during a rather

LEFT: Parnell vehemently denied accusations of Land League complicity in the Phoenix Park murders in the Times *and would be vindicated when the letters were exposed as the forgeries of Dublin journalist Richard Pigott.*

BELOW LEFT: Courtroom scene at the Special Inquiry Commission — Pigott is in the witness box, Parnell is seated right of center.

RIGHT: "Home Rule" — from the Weekly News *of January 30, 1886. Parnell threatens Salisbury with a poker saying, "You put down your foot upon Home Rule, did you? Well, my fine fellow you'll have to take it up again very much faster than you put it down."*

BELOW: Parnell's ancestral home, Avondale, Co. Wicklow.

one-sided hearing (Parnell and Katherine O'Shea did not defend themselves in court) public opinion was outraged. The somewhat puritanical nonconformist Protestants that made up so much of the Liberals' support were especially shocked. Gladstone and Parnell had become closely associated in their pursuit of Home Rule, and so Gladstone's own position, and hence the whole Home Rule project, was now under threat.

Parnell refused to take a temporary retirement, as advised by Gladstone and many others in his own party. After some tense meetings of the Irish MPs, and after a crucial intervention from the disapproving Catholic hierarchy, Parnell was deposed from the leadership. Showing increasingly irrational behavior, and having violently denounced the Liberals, he was defeated in a number of exhausting election campaigns during 1891. He still had allies, especially among Fenians who rallied to him as his rhetoric became more extreme, but public opinion had drifted away. His health, which had been poor for some time, began to deteriorate, and he died in the arms of his new wife Katherine in Brighton on October 6, 1891.

Parnell's achievement was manifold. He brought the energies of advanced nationalists and Fenians into constitutional politics and, by doing so, managed both to restrain them and enhance his own nationalist creden-

ABOVE: Parnell did not tell his party that he had been warned that Liberal support of Home Rule was dependent on his resignation. He was therefore unanimously re-elected as leader although, once Gladstone's message became known, a new contest was demanded.

RIGHT: "Parnell Party Portraits" from a supplement to the Weekly Irish Times of March 17, 1883. Parnell top left, MacCarthy top right; top row Healy, Biggar, O'Connor, Denton; second row Redmond, Dawson, Gray, O'Donnell; third row O'Brien, O'Kelly, Sullivan, Leamy; bottom row Lalor, Dillon, O'Sullivan, Harrington.

tials. He induced the Catholic hierarchy to endorse his goal of Home Rule, thus adding a powerful ally to his broad nationalist coalition; and he persuaded one of the two great British parties to accept Home Rule for Ireland as a principal policy goal for the first time. Perhaps most significantly he demonstrated that Irish men and women were capable of sustained, disciplined and effective political action — in and out of parliament. By doing so he showed many skeptics in Britain and the rest of the world that Ireland was capable and deserving of self-government. If he ultimately failed in his bid for Home Rule, the political movements he fostered laid the foundations of political experience and organization which would prove vital a generation later.

CHARLES S. PARNELL   JUSTIN M'CARTHY

TIMOTHY HEALY   JOSEPH G. BIGGAR   THOMAS P. O'CONNOR   THOMAS SEXTON

JOHN E. REDMOND   CHARLES DAWSON   EDMUND D. GRAY   FRANK H. O'DONNELL

WM. O'BRIEN   JAMES O'KELLY   TIMOTHY D. SULLIVAN   EDMUND LEAMY

INDEPENDENCE & BEYOND

PREVIOUS PAGE: A scene from the Irish Civil War.

ABOVE: Parnell's funeral was a magnificent affair, with crowds thronging the roads of Dublin from early morning waiting to pay their respects to their "Uncrowned King." This is Sackville Street (now O'Connell Street) and the cortege is on its way to Glasnevin Cemetery.

ABOVE RIGHT: John Redmond in Vanity Fair, *July 7, 1904. Redmond led the Home Rule Party through the long haul to the third Home Rule Bill in 1914. His life's work ended in tatters as World War I suspended the act's implementation for so long that events passed it by.*

BELOW RIGHT: John Dillon led the anti-Parnellite majority of the Home Rule Party in the late 1890s until its re-unification under Redmond in 1900. He briefly took over once again after the death of Redmond in March 1918.

Between 1891 and 1949 Ireland changed utterly. At the start of the period most of the Irish people were dissatisfied with British government, but sought Home Rule rather than complete independence. The vast majority simply wanted equality of status and a much greater degree of autonomy within the British Empire. However, 30 years later Ireland was in the grip of a vicious armed struggle between the British Army and the IRA, who wished to rid Ireland of British rule of any kind. Except for a sizeable minority of Protestants (largely in Ulster) most Irishmen and Irishwomen now wanted complete separation. This chapter will seek to explain this change of heart, before going on to chart the path to independence itself and to examine the development of Ireland from partition to the declaration of the republic.

PARLIAMENTARY NATIONALISM IN THE 1890S

The death of Parnell in 1891 left a vacuum at the heart of Irish parliamentary politics for a decade. By 1892 the Irish Parliamentary Party had split into a small minority of nine Parnellites under John Redmond and an anti-Parnellite majority of 72, first under Justin MacCarthy and then, after 1896, John Dillon. At this time there was a further split over the role of the Catholic Church in the party and the degree of independence that should be allowed to individual members and local committees. The majority, while not anti-Catholic, wished the party to continue to be centralized, essentially secular and free from the control of the clergy. A minority led by Tim Healy

sought a strong voice for the Catholic hierarchy and greater independence for individual MPs. However, the personal animosity between John Dillon and William O'Brien on the one hand, and Tim Healy on the other, also added to the infighting.

Yet Irish political activity and parliamentary nationalism were not quite as ineffective as they are sometimes made out to be — even if the parliamentary party itself showed a lack of leadership. When Gladstone was returned to power for the last time in 1892, he manfully tried to steer another Home Rule Bill through parliament. The bill passed the Commons in 1893 but, as everyone expected, it was defeated in the Lords. This blow finally led to Gladstone's resignation from the leadership of the Liberals in May 1894. To the dismay of the Irish Party, his replacement, Lord Rosebery, was far from committed to Home Rule, and talked of the need for England to be convinced of its justice and equity before it could proceed. Given that the Liberals were removed from power for a decade in 1895 by a coalition of Conservatives and Liberal Unionists, their attitude to Home Rule probably mattered little. This lack of Liberal support was nonetheless demoralizing for the Irish Parliamentary Party. Already riven by internal squabbling, many members (including Redmond and Healy) now became unsure as to the value of the Liberal alliance which had been their lodestar since the 1880s and the main reason for getting rid of Parnell. Even if the Liberals were to return to government (which they were not to do until 1906), there was now no guarantee they would pursue Home Rule with any real vigor or commitment.

Despite its lack of achievement, the Home Rule Party continued to maintain its considerable representation at Westminster. After the 1895 election the anti-Parnellites still held 71 seats and the Parnellites 11, but their influence both at Westminster and in Ireland waned. By 1900 the party was reunited under the leadership of John Redmond. This was partly due to the pressure of William O'Brien's extremely popular United Irish League (UIL), which had been formed in 1898 as both a focus for further land agitation and as an umbrella organization for other nationalist groups. The party excluded Healy and was brought under the control of the UIL. From the outside this looked like a takeover by the UIL, whose branches served as the constituency organizations with the power to choose candidates, but as the leaders of the parliamentary party soon became the leaders of the UIL, the takeover was really the other way round.

A decade of unseemly rows and backbiting had given the impression that Ireland's interests were not being well-served by its parliamentarians. To many of their voters the Irish MPs seemed more interested in their places at Westminster, their internal feuds and their support for the Liberals than in the independence of Ireland. However under Redmond the Home Rule Party regained some of its old discipline and effectiveness in the 1900s, but it took a long time to recover its influence.

CULTURAL NATIONALISM 1892–1907

To fill this breach there arose a number of organizations which sought to develop and express Irish nationality culturally rather than politically. Their goals were to arrest and reverse English and materialistic influences — often seen as virtually the same thing — so that Ireland could develop its own distinctive and ancient Gaelic identity. Highly influential in this broad cultural revival was the Gaelic Athletic Association (GAA), founded back in 1884 by Michael Cusack, and the Gaelic League, which had important political aspects and was founded in 1893 by Douglas Hyde, Eoin MacNeill and Fr. Eugene O'Growney. The literary activities of these two bodies will be dealt with in Chapter 5.

The GAA and the Gaelic League, while both were conspicuously non-political, inspired a cultural and artistic revival which inevitably had political implications. Their aim was to train the Irish people to turn away mentally from England even in if they could not do so politically — or as Hyde put it in his famous essay, *The necessity for de-Anglicising Ireland:*

"I would earnestly appeal to every one, whether Unionist or Nationalist, who wishes to see the Irish nation produce its best — and surely whatever our politics are we all wish that — to set his face against this constant running to England for our books, literature, music, games, fashions and ideas. I appeal to every one whatever his politics — for this is no political matter — to do his best to help the Irish race to develop in future along Irish lines, even at the risk of encouraging national aspirations, because

upon Irish lines alone can the Irish race once more become what it was of yore — one of the most artistic, literary, and charming people of Europe."

Hyde, a member of the Church of Ireland, was an amiable, eccentric reactionary, who was motivated as much by a distaste for the modern as a dislike of all things English. Hyde stressed that he did not wish to:

" . . . protest against imitating what is best in the English people, for that would be absurd, but rather to show the folly of neglecting what is Irish, and hastening to adopt, pell-mell, and indiscriminately, everything that is English, simply because it is English."

However, this seemingly measured approach often gave way to preoccupations that verged on the plainly ridiculous, such as Hyde's aversion to trousers as an English invention which should be rejected in favor of the traditional Irish knee-breech. In retrospect, the GAA could be similarly quirky. It sought to replace all English games, such as football, cricket and rugby, with native "Gaelic" ones such as hurling and Gaelic football. It even went so far as to ban its members from playing these English games — despite the fact that some of them had a longer history in Ireland than the "Gaelic" sports recently invented by the GAA, such as Gaelic football. During the 1890s, the GAA expanded throughout the country and infused a whole generation of young Irishmen with a sense of national pride in a Gaelic resurgence. From the start the association had been infiltrated by Fenians and

IRB members at the highest levels and, like the Gaelic League, the GAA would eventually provide many of the Irish Volunteers after 1913.

The Gaelic League's basic goals were twofold: to protect and revive the Irish language, and to foster Gaelic Irish literary culture. The former would take effect through the establishment of local branches providing language instruction, while the latter was pursued through the rediscovery of ancient Celtic mythology and the collection of surviving fragments of peasant folklore, especially from the west. By 1902 the league had nearly 400 branches and had secured the teaching of Irish in national schools. The league also became a focus of middle class local life, with its drama groups — Feiseanna — and classes in dancing and history, as well language. This urban, middle class and usually Catholic world rejected all "West Britons" and Shoneens ("little johnnies" who supported the Castle), and its desire to create an Irish social atmosphere included enthusiasm for Irish music and song, Irish prayers, Irish names, Irish education, Irish-speaking servants and visits to Irish-speaking districts. The latter were so frequent that by the time of J. M. Synge's visits to the Aran Islands at the turn of the century, the numbers of language students there were enough to persuade the islanders that the chief occupation of the outside world was Gaelic studies!

Such support for all things Irish, however laudable, also included rejection of all things un-Irish (which did not only mean things English). This attitude often created a narrow-minded social straightjacket which was deadening for cosmopolitan and European-minded artists such as James Joyce. In conjunction with the traditional conservatism of Catholic Ireland, this approach led Joyce to dub Dublin the "centre of paralysis." His short story *The Dead* depicts the social pressure which the desire to recover Gaelic culture exerted. Even writing book reviews for an English newspaper and taking holidays in Europe instead of in the Gaelic-speaking west were both frowned upon.

Political nationalism as such was not part of the league's official remit, but it was obvious that the league's ethos could fit neatly with advanced Irish nationalism. Many people joined at least partly for political reasons, and many who did not were politicized by its activities. Indeed the Gaelic League fulfiled a vital role in late-19th century Irish nationalism. Many theorists held that all true nations must have their own distinct language and culture. European nationalists (such as Mazzini, the father of Italian unification) even went so far as to question Ireland's claims to nationhood because it shared so closely the literary and linguistic culture of Britain. Young enthusiasts in the league hoped that their cultural revival would show Ireland to be distinct from England and so bolster her claim to true nationhood.

Thus a broad sense of political nationalism infused the Celtic revival of the 1890s and 1900s and gave many of its adherents a common purpose. Intense disagreements about the way forward for the cultural revival divided it into two rival camps. On the one hand there was the Anglo-Irish literary revival of W. B. Yeats, George Moore, Lady Gregory and J. M. Synge, which created a national literature based on native Irish and Celtic themes in English (although often in an English which consciously mirrored the rhythms and constructions of Gaelic). On the other hand, there was the Irish-Ireland movement, as championed by D. P. Moran in his influential paper *The Leader*, which sought to replace completely English with Irish as the spoken and literary language of the country.

This Irish-Ireland movement gained increasing cohesion from Arthur Griffith's *Sinn Fein* ("ourselves") movement, which had started life as *Cumann na nGaedheal* in 1900. Many members were fundamentally republican separatists, but officially the movement called for an independent Irish parliament under the crown — in other words, greater separation than was envisaged by Home Rulers and a similar constitutional status, in theory, to "Grattan's Parliament" of 1782–1800. Of course this was based on a horrible misreading of the real status of that parliament, which was controlled through corruption by Britain just as it had been before 1782, but the formula

ABOVE LEFT: The Gaelic **An Claidheamh Soluis** *newspaper was founded in 1889. Here its June 13, 1903, issue shows the full range of distinctly Gaelic cultural and social activities.*

ABOVE RIGHT: Douglas Hyde, a founder of the Gaelic League and a central figure in the cultural revival. His essay, **The necessity for de-Anglicising Ireland,** *written in 1892 was highly influential.*

RIGHT: Arthur Griffith founded Sinn Fein in midst of widespread Irish opposition to the Boer War.

ABOVE: John Millington Synge, the brilliant young playwright of the literary revival, died tragically young in 1909 of Hodgkinson's disease. He is probably most famous for his controversial play **The Playboy of the Western World.**

provided a vague enough rallying point to encompass a wide range of advanced nationalist opinion.

Cumann na nGaedheal drew much of its energy from opposition to the Boer War in South Africa and widespread disgust for Britain's treatment of the Boers (a particularly shameful consequence of this war was the invention by the British of the concentration camp). To many Irish eyes, the Boers were fellow sufferers of Imperial oppression, and it is difficult to overstate the effect of this distant war on nationalist opinion in Ireland. By the time Cumann na nGaedheal had amalgamated with the Dungannon Clubs to form Sinn Fein, Griffith was calling for non-cooperation with the British government and the withdrawal of Irish MPs from Westminster to form an Irish government in Dublin. His model, which was based on the Hungarians' success in establishing their own parliament in the face of Austrian opposition, seemed fanciful at the time, but it would prove highly effective in 1919.

The main rallying point for the Anglo-Irish literary revival was the Irish Literary Theatre, founded by Yeats, Lady Gregory, George Moore and Edward Martyn in

1898. This broke new ground in the style and subject matter of its plays, and by 1905 it a had evolved into the Irish National Theatre Society at the Abbey Theatre. The theater was enmeshed in controversy from the start. Yeats's *The Countess Cathleen*, performed in the first season, portrayed devils tempting poverty-stricken peasants with gold in return for their souls, and the Countess Cathleen herself succumbing to a Faustian pact to save them. Such themes were not looked on favorably by Dublin's Catholic middle classes. Tensions rose again in 1903 over Synge's comedy *The Shadow of the Glen*. The idea of a bored young country wife running away from her older husband with a tinker was too much for Arthur Griffith, who called the play a lie in his paper *The United Irishman*. "All of us know that Irish women are the most virtuous in the world," he declared.

There was greater controversy to come in 1907, with Synge's *The Playboy of the Western World*. Synge's great play depicted a sexually-confident peasant woman attempting to seduce a young man who, after thinking he has killed his father, becomes idolized by the remote western community to which he has fled. The play caused riots for a week; it went against the ideal of a simple but virtuous peasantry embodying the true nobility of the Irish people, a notion which had become dear to the urban nationalists of Dublin. Of course, unlike Synge who had spent three summers on the beautiful but bleak Aran Islands, most of the audience had no idea of the hard, cruel and melancholy life endured in these remote parts of the west — but it was Irish image rather than reality that was at stake. After centuries of negative commentary, the Irish peasant must now be shown capable of dignified self-government, rather than superstition and uncontrolled passion as explored by the play.

Despite these controversies, the Irish National Theatre Society was also a significant ally of the nationalist enterprise. While never accepting the doctrine that art should be subservient to politics, many of its plays were nevertheless highly nationalist. In 1900 the theater put on the first modern play in Irish — Douglas Hyde's *Casadh an tSugan* (The Twisting of the Rope). But most notable is Yeats's *Cathleen ni Houlihan* (1902), in which a woman representing Ireland itself (a common motif in Celtic myth and the literary revival) persuades young Irish men to seek everlasting glory by dying for her. "They that have red cheeks will have pale cheeks for my sake," predicts Cathleen ni Houlihan and, much later, Yeats worried that his youthful nationalism had been too reckless. "Did that play of mine send out/Certain men the English shot?" he wondered.

The impact of the Yeats's play, and the Celtic revival as a whole, was certainly intense among small sections of the population, and it undoubtedly did influence the intellectuals and writers (especially Patrick Pearse) who led the Easter Rising in 1916. We should not forget, however, that much of this debate and controversy was of little consequence to the everyday lives of most Irish men and women — at least before 1916. Far more Dubliners went to the English-style music halls than ever crossed the threshold of the Abbey Theatre. Additionally, as the resounding defeat of a Sinn Fein candidate (the ex-Home Rule MP Charles Dolan) in a 1908 by-election demonstrated, Sinn Fein was in no danger of ousting the dominant Irish Parliamentary Party while an old-style Home Rule Bill had any chance of success.

In the countryside especially, these political debates had limited impact. The conservative instincts of small farmers and peasants were focused on consolidating their holdings rather than the latest play by Synge. The inhabitants of remote western areas like the Aran Islands were more likely to be bewildered than inspired with patriotism at the sight of Lady Gregory striding across their barren landscape in search of native Irish speakers.

CONSTRUCTIVE UNIONISM

Since 1891 there had been a number of private individuals and government officials working to ensure that no Irishmen felt the need to have "pale cheeks" for Ireland again. These men, often Conservative and Unionist by instinct, were trying to improve the economic and social condition of Ireland, to remove the grievances which they thought lay at the root of advanced nationalism. Essentially they sought a lasting solution to the land question and to endemic western poverty, neither of which, as William O'Brien's Plan of Campaign had shown, had been fully solved by the 1890s. Evictions and high rents were generally a thing of the past, but most farmers still rented rather than owned their farms. In retrospect the activities of these "constructive Unionists" seem doomed to failure, but this was not seen as the case at the time. Their efforts between 1891 and 1906 left a significant mark on the economy and social structure of Ireland, and many nationalists were seriously worried that they would "kill Home Rule with kindness."

While Parnell was engaged in his last ditch attempt to re-establish his leadership of Irish nationalism, the British Conservative government was quietly inaugurating a period of reform. The chief secretary, Arthur Balfour, had promised a period of resolute government, but in reality he moved away from the previous coercive approach to Ireland. The Balfour Act of August 5, 1891, set up the Congested Districts Board (CDB) which tried to improve the infrastructure, industry and agriculture of the poorest parts of western Ireland. It built roads, harbors and bridges, encouraged local industries (especially fishing), and bought-up land (two million acres of it) to reorganize the most crowded areas. The act also increased the amount of government money available for land purchase to £33 million, accelerating the gradual process of land purchase started by Gladstone. The light railways which were built to provide employment in the near-famine year of 1890 also began to open up the west.

Under the auspices of Arthur Balfour's brother Gerald, a further measure of land reform was passed in 1896, and in 1898 Irish local government was radically altered and placed on a genuinely democratic footing. The new, wide franchise for the county and local district councils included women for the first time and ensured that local government passed from Protestant landlords to the Catholic middle classes. These measures were not without their problems. Local government may have become more democratic, but it often also became corrupt. Many of the railways built were economically unviable and fell into disuse. Only about a tenth of families in the Congested Districts received significant benefit by the re-distribution of land, and rates of emigration from the west remained very high. But the reforms represent positive engagement with deep-seated problems, even if they failed to produce most of the long term results hoped for.

Perhaps the key figure in Constructive Unionism was Sir Horace Plunkett. After 10 years as a successful rancher in Wyoming, he returned to Ireland to start the co-operative movement in 1889. This tried to combat agricultural backwardness by encouraging an ethos of self-help among groups of local farmers. Co-operatives supplied information, fertilizers and equipment. Their land banks allowed farmers to take out loans to improve their holdings, and co-operative creameries improved the standard of dairy products while cutting out the middle man. By 1894 Plunkett had set up the Irish Agricultural Organisation Society as an umbrella body for the rapidly-multiplying co-operatives, and by 1899 he had persuaded the government to form the Irish Agricultural Department (with himself as vice-president). This held a wide brief covering technical education, fisheries and public health, as well as all aspects of agricultural improvement.

Plunkett was an independent-minded Unionist MP for South Dublin. He later accepted the idea of dominion status as a suitable compromise, but by this time he had managed to upset both Unionists and Nationalists with his frank opinions. When his *Ireland in The New Century* was published in 1904, its honest and penetrating analysis caused a storm. Ireland was so obsessed by the idea that political solutions would solve its agricultural economic problems, he argued, that it had lost the ability to help itself. Without excusing the historical role of England in contributing to Irish poverty, Plunkett argued that it was time Ireland started sorting out its own problems instead of constantly blaming England and assuming such efforts were pointless without Home Rule. The following passage is a good example of Plunkett's uncompromising attitude:

"It is a peculiarity of destructive criticism that, unlike charity, it generally begins and ends abroad; and those who cultivate the gentle art are seldom given to morbid introspection. Our prodigious ignorance about ourselves has not been blissful. Mistaking self-assertion for self-knowledge, we have presented the pathetic spectacle of a people casting the blame for their shortcomings on another people, yet bearing the consequences themselves. The national habit of living in the past seems to give us a present without achievement, a future without hope. The conclusion was long ago forced upon me that whatever may have been true of the past, the chief responsibility for the remoulding of our national life rests now with ourselves, and that in the last analysis the problem of Irish ineffectiveness at home is in the main a problem of character — and of Irish character."

ABOVE: "Easter Eggs," a color cartoon from Weekly Freeman and National Press of April 18, 1903. Watched by "Pat," Wyndham (famous for his influential Land Act of that year) hatches eggs labeled "Home Rule" and "Irish Land Bill." The caption reads: "Pat: 'I wonder if these eggs will grow up alright.'"

Such bracing appeals from the son of an Anglo-Irish Protestant aristocrat were unlikely to win Plunkett friends among Catholic nationalists, especially as he was also critical of the influence of the Catholic Church on Irish moral fiber. Once the Liberals returned to power in 1906, his position became untenable.

The high point of Constructive Unionism was the Land Conference, which proved a remarkable moment of co-operation between Unionist landlords and nationalist representatives of the tenants. Responding to the private initiative of Captain John Shawe-Taylor, the conference met in December 1902 and swiftly produced a short report which became the basis of the famous Wyndham Land Act of 1903. Its members were John Redmond, William O'Brien, George Russell, Timothy Harrington, Colonel Nugent Everard, Colonel Hutcheson-Poe and the Earls of Mayo and Dunraven (chairman). The act itself encouraged landlords to sell off entire estates by giving them a 12 percent cash bonus on top of the market price. It also allowed tenants to buy on easy terms stretching over 68½ years at only 3¼ percent interest. An amendment was needed in 1909 to rectify problems and the act was not without its critics, notably Davitt and Dillon, who criticized the hefty 12 percent bonus for landlords. But it was the Wyndham Land Act more than any other which led to the wholesale transfer of property from landlord to tenant. Between 1903 and independence around 11 million acres changed hands: the Irish landlord system had finally died.

There were strong hopes that this method of civilized co-operation (labeled "conference plus business" by O'Brien) could be extended to other areas such as Catholic university education, and eventually the Home Rule question itself. Co-operation on wider issues proved impossible. Indeed, the success of this movement was to prove its undoing, as hard-liners on both sides had difficulty in coming to terms with its experiments. Most Unionists thought that the Protestant landlords involved in the conferences, such as Dunraven, were not representative of Unionist opinion and were too accommodating to nationalists and agrarian socialists.

Nationalists feared the possibility of "killing nationalism through kindness," while some simply could not comprehend well-meaning reform on the part of a small section of the Protestant Anglo-Irish elite without imagining sinister motives. The death knell of both Constructive Unionism and "conference plus business" was sounded by the devolution crisis of 1904. A Catholic undersecretary called Sir Antony MacDonnell had been working with Dunraven and his newly-formed Irish Reform Association of Irish landlords to develop plans for devolving certain financial and law-making powers to Irish councils. When the plans were published, most Unionists were outraged by what they thought amounted to a limited form of Home Rule. MacDonnell let it be known that their work had been authorized by Wyndham, and so Unionists jumped on Wyndham and forced his resignation.

The Constructive Unionist experiment came to an end with the resignation of Arthur Balfour (by then prime minister) in December 1905. It had obviously failed to bring mainstream Unionists and nationalists together, and it could be argued that the general rise in living standards over this period owed more to increasing agricultural prices and the adoption of the potato spray than to efforts of Plunkett, Wyndham or Balfour. However the Board of Agriculture, the co-operative movement and the CDB did bring some useful, if piecemeal, reforms which helped to alleviate poverty in Ireland; and in the Wyndham Land

Act the basis for a solution of the land issue was finally laid. Thus, in the countryside at least, a social and economic revolution had already taken place before the political one in 1919–21. Ironically, it was a revolution engineered largely by British Conservatives and Irish Unionists

UNIONISM AND ORANGEISM

As direct result of the devolution crisis, northern Unionists set up the Ulster Unionist Council in 1905 to co-ordinate opposition to Home Rule. This act was no more than a formal recognition of pre-existing divisions, but it was highly symbolic nonetheless. For not only did it signal their rejection of the conciliation techniques of Dunraven, Wyndham, Plunkett and O'Brien, it gave a clear message to the incoming Liberal government of January 1906 that Ulster would not have Home Rule. Ulster's opposition to Home Rule had been apparent since the first Home Rule Bill of 1886. That year had seen the worst Irish riots of the entire century in Belfast, and many Catholics were killed as working class Protestants gave full vent to their fears and bigotry.

The Orange Order had long regained its support after a lull in the 1830s and 1840s and it now began to attract the Protestant Ascendancy as well as the lower classes. Colonel Edward Saunderson emerged as the leader of the Ulster Unionist MPs within the Conservative Party, and during the next Home Rule crisis of 1893 (which also saw serious Protestant rioting in Belfast) he organized the Ulster Defence Union. The 1893 Home Rule Bill was defeated in the Lords, and the decade of Conservative government which followed (1895–1905) gave little cause for concern to Ulster Protestants until the devolution crisis of 1904–05. Their reaction to this, and to a new Liberal government under Campbell-Bannerman, was entirely predictable from events that had gone before.

The intense fear in Ulster of Home Rule merely reflected deep divisions in both identity and perceptions of self-interest between Protestant Loyalists and Catholic nationalists. These divisions had historical roots in the religious warfare of the 17th century. In the Protestant version of events, the Catholic massacres of Protestants in 1641 took their place alongside the Protestant victories at the Boyne and the siege of Londonderry 50 years later, to provide a powerful moral tale. This tale impressed the need for constant Protestant vigilance in defense of their lives, their rights and their religion, and it showed, they thought, that with courage and with God's help they could and would be victorious again — just as they were in the 1690s.

The divisions also had more recent aspects. It is often listed as an achievement of both O'Connell and, to a lesser extent, Parnell that they used the organization and influence of the Catholic Church for their nationalist ends. This policy was not without its drawbacks. The more Home Rule became associated with Catholicism, the more it would lose support among Irish Protestants. In their very different ways, Young Ireland and Butt's Home Government Association had visions of a united Ireland which saw religion as secondary. But by the 1880s and 1890s Catholicism and nationalism had become firmly united in most Protestants' minds.

Economics also divided Ulster (and especially Belfast) from the rest of Ireland. Belfast had grown enormously in size and prosperity under the Union and both workers and business leaders alike saw the link as vital to their continued success. A population of around 13,000 in 1783 had jumped to over 250,000 by 1891, and by the 1890s the port of Belfast was second only to London and Liverpool in terms of the value of its trade. This impressive commercial success was firmly tied to the British market, which Belfast relied upon for the importation of raw materials such as coal, iron and steel and the exportation of linen, ships and engineered goods.

Of course it was not just in Ulster that Unionism was found. Many Irishmen and women from all over the country, including many Catholics, saw themselves as firmly entrenched in the British Empire. They felt no contradiction in being both Irish and, in a wider imperial sense, part of the Britain and its culture. The British Army and Royal Navy contained disproportionately large numbers of Catholic Irishmen, mainly in the lower ranks, while Anglo-Irish Protestants filled the higher ranks. The Duke of Wellington, Sir Garnett Wolseley, Lord Roberts, Lord Kitchener and Lord Montgomery all came from Anglo-Irish stock. Indeed many members of the aristocratic and military establishment had a foot on either side of the Irish Sea, and this convinced them that Ireland was an integral part of United Kingdom. Such strong convictions led to committed (and even illegal) elite British support for Irish Unionists during the crisis years of 1910–1914.

Southern Unionism differed from the Ulster variety. Thinly spread and predominantly Anglican, southern loyalists, and especially elite landowners, often simply withdrew into a private world of horses and hunting on their rapidly shrinking estates. When they did engage in politics, they were often forced to take a more constructive and conciliatory approach to nationalists as they were unable to retreat behind the idea of partition.

Thus there were a variety of elements to Unionism, ranging from the violent popular Orangeism of working-class Belfast Protestants, to the sturdy Presbyterian commercial middle classes of eastern Ulster, to the Anglican Anglo-Irish Ascendancy landlords. Many of the latter undoubtedly viewed the sectarian rioting and vulgar prejudice of Belfast with distaste, while many Presbyterians of Scottish descent continued to resent the elitism of the Anglo-Irish Ascendancy; but the prospect of a Catholic-dominated parliament in Dublin focused minds. The majority of Protestants came increasingly to the view that the only way to preserve their own rights (and the well-being of Ireland as a whole) was to join forces with each other in defence of the Union.

In 1906 Home Rule was not imminent, but some significant Irish measures were enacted by the new Liberal government, such as the Evicted Tenants Act of 1907, the Land Act of 1909 which gave the government powers of compulsory purchase, and the Irish Universities Act of 1908. The latter finally satisfied Catholic demands by

The calm before the storm — Ireland in the early years of the 20th century may have been a political cauldron ready to boil over, but for most Irishmen and women it was a much better place to live in than it had been in the 19th century. ABOVE and BELOW: Scenes of Cork, the center of which would suffer dreadfully at the hands of the Black and Tans in 1920. ABOVE LEFT: The harbor at Kingstown, which would be renamed Dun Laoghaire after the British left. BELOW LEFT: Dublin's strawberry beds.

founding a National University with colleges in Dublin, Cork and Galway largely under Catholic control. However, many Liberals were still unsure of the merits of Home Rule after the havoc it had wreaked on their party in 1886, and with their large majority they could afford to ignore it for the time being. A half-hearted attempt was made to introduce a limited measure of devolution with an Irish Council Bill in 1907, but this was dropped after opposition from Redmond. Unionists could still just about breath easily.

CRISIS 1910–14

The Irish situation had changed by the end of 1910, however. The second general election of that year left 74 MPs of the Irish Parliamentary Party (and 10 Irish independents) holding the balance of power between 271 Liberals, 273 Conservatives and Liberal Unionists, and 42 Socialists. The two elections of 1910 were the result of a serious constitutional clash between the Commons and the Lords. Traditionally, the unelected House of Lords, could veto any legislation coming from the democratically elected Commons (as it had done with Home Rule in 1893), but this autocratic elitist behavior was seen as increasingly unacceptable in a new democratic age. The inevitable clash between the reforming Liberal government in the Commons and the Tory-dominated House of Lords came over the controversial 1909 budget, which raised a number of taxes to pay for state pensions and other social reforms. After the Lords rejected it, elections were called to provide the government with a mandate to curb its powers. However, it was only after the threat of a mass creation of new peers to force a Liberal majority in

the Lords that a compromise was reached. By the Parliament Act of 1911 new legislation could only be vetoed in two successive sessions by the Lords, in effect thus giving them the power to delay legislation for about two years.

These events derived added intensity from the explosively emotive issue of Irish Home Rule hovering in the background, for it was clear that once the Lords' power of veto had been curtailed, Home Rule would have a realistic chance of succeeding for the first time. After some foot-dragging by the Liberal government, now under the leadership of Herbert Henry Asquith, the third Home Rule Bill was presented to Parliament in April 1912. By January 1913 it passed the Commons for the first time by 367 votes to 257, and although predictably defeated in the Lords, it seemed like only a matter of time before it must come into operation. The inevitable delay, however, was to cause enormous problems for Asquith and Redmond; it allowed opposition to the bill to organize and passed the initiative to the Unionists.

Protestant Ulster's resistance to the bill was swift and impressive. In 1910 the Ulster Unionist party had acquired two formidable new leaders, Sir Edward Carson and James Craig. Carson, who took over from Walter Long in 1910 (the previous leader Saunderson having died in 1906), was a brilliant lawyer and the Liberal Unionist MP for Dublin University. He had served in Conservative governments and had powerful connections in the Conservative party, which had even considered him for its leadership at one point. Craig, who would eventually take over from Carson in 1921, was a successful Belfast stockbroker and whiskey manufacturer who had

fought in the Boer War before becoming Unionist MP for East Down. By September 1911 they had already laid plans for a provisional government in Ulster should Home Rule come into effect, and by 1912 the British Conservatives were firmly committed to backing them all the way. In language that seems shocking in its implications today, the Conservative leader Bonar Law declared:

"There are things stronger than parliamentary majorities . . . I can imagine no lengths to which Ulster will go . . . in which they will not be supported by the overwhelming majority of the British people."

Such arrogant disdain for democracy was inspired partly by the Tory belief that the Liberals had somehow entered a devious agreement with the Irish MPs to emasculate the Lords in return for Home Rule. Still smarting from the successful assault on the Lords, the Tories also felt that a Home Rule Bill which relied on Irish votes was somehow illegitimate. This bizarre reasoning, of course, only served to highlight the validity of the nationalists' point about the injustice of the Union. For if an MP from Mayo did not carry the same weight as his fellow MP from Surrey, then the whole concept of a United Kingdom was a sham.

In the increasingly emotional crisis years of 1912–14 such logicality counted for little. In order to show they meant business about not having Home Rule, the Ulster Protestants organized a mass demonstration of opposition for September 28, 1912, which they declared "Ulster Day." As part of the proceedings, about 220,000 Ulstermen signed the following Solemn League and Covenant:

ABOVE LEFT: "The Mandate" from the **Weekly Freeman, National Press and Irish Agriculturist** *of February 5, 1910. Asquith and his cabinet are all in armor. The Prime Minister says: "Behold our new charter of freedom. First and foremost the Veto of the Lords must go. They can no longer be allowed to kill the Legislation of the People." At the time, the removal of this veto seemed to open the way to Home Rule.*

ABOVE: Dublin barrister Sir Edward Carson took over leadership of the Ulster Unionist party in 1910, which was firmly set against Home Rule.

"Being convinced in our consciences that Home Rule would be disastrous to the material well-being of Ulster as well as to the whole of Ireland, subversive of our civil and religious freedom, destructive of our citizenship and perilous to the unity of the Empire, we . . . men of Ulster, loyal subjects of His Gracious Majesty King George V, humbly relying on God whom our fathers in days of stress and trial confidently trusted, do hereby pledge ourselves in solemn Covenant throughout this our time of threatened calamity to stand by one another in defending for ourselves and our children our cherished position of equal citizenship in the United Kingdom and in using all means which may be found necessary to defeat the present conspiracy to set up a Home Rule Parliament in Ireland. And in the event of such a Parliament being forced upon us we further solemnly and mutually pledge ourselves to refuse to recognize its authority. In sure confidence that God will defend the right we hereto subscribe our names."

Ireland was drifting toward crisis, and the logic of the

situation was beginning to point toward some form of partition, but Redmond and Asquith still thought the Ulster Unionists were bluffing. Ulster as a whole contained almost as many Catholics as Protestants, and neither Unionists nor nationalists really wanted partition. Southern Unionists, such as Carson, were particularly averse to the idea. Partition would leave them a very small minority in an overwhelmingly Catholic south. In fact Carson, in one sense, was bluffing about partition, for he thought Ireland without the wealth and industry of Ulster would be unviable — so he hoped Ulster intransigence would destroy Home Rule altogether. However, many northern Protestants were beginning to give up on the south as a lost cause and considered the exemption of some part of Ulster from Home Rule as their best hope. By January 1913, there was no excuse for nationalist wishful thinking about Ulster's intentions: an Ulster Volunteer Force of 100,000 men was formed and money for arms began to flow in. The strength of Nationalist opinion would not allow Redmond to consider partition. In one sense, why should he have done? The Home Rule Bill would be law by 1914, and many argued that the Ulster Protestants would just have to accept it. Nationalists and Liberals knew, or at least should have known, that it would not be that easy.

The increasing sense of crisis was heightened in the late summer of 1913 by the outbreak of massive industrial unrest in Dublin. The dispute is inextricably linked to the names of two remarkable men: James Connolly and James Larkin. Larkin, the Liverpool-born son of Irish immigrants, was a charismatic and confrontational orator who had been stirring up the revolutionary consciousness of the Irish proletariat since his arrival in Belfast in 1907. His trades union activities had even (very briefly) overcome the religious divides in the factories and shipyards of that city, but he ultimately failed to produce a non-sectarian, working-class solidarity in the north. He came south to Dublin, and in the following year founded the Irish Transport and General Worker's Union (ITGWU). Connolly, born in Edinburgh, was the self-educated, philosopher-worker of Irish socialism. After founding the Irish Socialist Republican Party in 1896, poverty forced his emigration to America in 1902, but he returned in 1910 to become the most prominent figure in the ITGWU after Larkin and the intellectual leader of the Irish labor movement. In August 1913, the

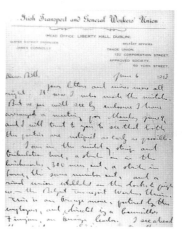

ABOVE: Letter from James Connolly, the patron saint of Irish socialism and organizer for the ITGWU in Belfast, to William O'Brien regarding union affairs in the north, June 16, 1913.

BELOW: A poster for the October 18, 1913, issue of the Labour newspaper, the Daily Herald, *relating to the Dublin strike. The "Lockout," as it was popularly known after employers locked their employees out of their premises, was a titanic struggle between capital and labor and a traumatic event for many working-class Dubliners.*

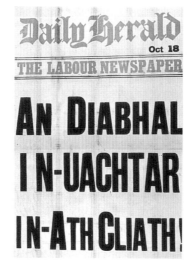

ITGWU called a strike after William Martin Murphy, the leader of a federation of business leaders, refused to recognize the union. The strike initially centered on Murphy's own Dublin Tramways company, but it soon spread as employers locked out 25,000 union members. It became an epic struggle between the forces of labor and capital.

One of the reasons for the strike was the appalling condition of the poor in Dublin. Its slums were among the worst in Europe, and their overcrowding and inadequate sanitation gave the city one of the highest mortality rates in the western world. The fact that many of these slum landlords, and indeed Murphy himself, were prominent figures in the Irish Parliamentary Party, brought home to many Dubliners the fact that Home Rule under such leaders was unlikely to improve their lot. The Home Rule Party was largely a rural and conservative party which had never shown much interest in urban improvement and social reform. Indeed, the big business and brewing interests within the party disliked the substance of Lloyd George's reforming budget of 1909 and only supported it because of the crisis it would provoke with the Lords. The efforts of municipal government in English cities like Birmingham and Liverpool in areas such as housing, sanitation and public health put Home Rulers in the corrupt Dublin corporation to shame.

Thus, during the lockout the Parliamentary party (and the Catholic Church) effectively lined up behind the employers. Riots and police brutality led to a number of deaths and scores of injuries. Sympathetic British workers sent food ships at the beginning, but by January 1914 half-starved workers began drifting back to work. Effectively the employers had won, but they had failed to break the union and the near-anarchy on Dublin's streets added to an atmosphere of social and political crisis. A significant side effect of the strike was the creation by Connolly in October 1913 of a small Irish Citizen Army to defend the workers. This was fairly insignificant at the time and nearly disappeared after the strike, but it was revamped by the future playwright Sean O'Casey, and its hard core of 300 or so men went on to play a crucial role in the Easter Rising. By the end of the year there was yet another unauthorized military body in Ireland. Responding to the challenge of the Ulster Volunteers, which many nationalists admired, Eoin MacNeill, Bulmer

ABOVE: James Larkin was the charismatic leader of the Irish trade union movement who led the strikers during the lockout of 1913. This statue of him stands on O'Connell Street in Dublin, a short distance from that of O'Connell himself.

ABOVE RIGHT: James Connolly, a leading figure in the ITGWU and the intellectual leader of Irish socialism, led the Irish Citizen Army in the Easter Rising of 1916. He would be executed by firing squad while seated in a chair as his wounds prevented him from standing.

BELOW: A police escort for vans delivering strike-breaking goods in the Belfast Strike of 1907. This was Larkin's first attempt to stir up industrial unrest in Ireland. After the failure he moved to Dublin where he was later instrumental in organizing the famous Dublin strike of 1913.

During the crisis years of 1913 — 14, when the third Home Rule Bill was making its way through parliament, volunteering became hugely popular all over Ireland. The two main groups of citizen-soldiers were the Ulster Volunteers in the north set up by Carson and Craig, and the Irish Volunteers established by nationalists in the south.

Hobson (another playwright) and Michael Rahilly founded the Irish Volunteers.

These were unusual times, and by the spring of 1914, when the Home Rule Bill was about to pass the Commons for the last time, the threat of civil war loomed. Asquith, between a rock and a hard place, was forced to concede the need for an accommodation for Ulster. In the Commons on March 9 he argued:

". . . on the one hand, if Home Rule as embodied in this Bill is carried now, there is, I regret to say it, but nobody can deny it, in Ulster the prospect of acute dissension and even of civil strife. On the other hand, if at this stage Home Rule were to be shipwrecked, or permanently mutilated, or indefinitely postponed, there is in Ireland as a whole an equally formidable outlook."

There was, he asserted, an obvious need for compromise and moderation which, "must involve, in the first place, on the side of our opponents the acceptance of a Home Rule Legislature and Executive in Dublin, and, on the other hand, on the side of our supporters, some form of special treatment for the Ulster minority over and above any of the safeguards which are contained in this Bill."

One of the reasons Asquith had for seeking a compromise was the desire to avoid coercion. There was an instinctive revulsion among most British politicians at the idea of using British troops to force loyal Ulster subjects to submit to a Home Rule parliament at gun point. Asquith also knew that Unionist sympathy within the army made the use of force against Ulster a risky strategy. The Ulster Volunteers were by now commanded by a retired British general, Sir George Richardson, whose name had been suggested by no less a figure than Field Marshal Lord Roberts. When 57 out of 70 officers at the Curragh army base offered to resign their commissions rather than march against Ulster, it became clear that parts of the army might mutiny if ordered to impose Home Rule by force. Aside from the absurdity of the Commander-in-Chief of the Army in Ireland, Sir Arthur Paget, giving his officers the opportunity to express their opinions in the first place (the British Army was not normally known for such communal decision-making), this was an unprecedented breakdown in political authority. Asquith, perhaps understandably, was desperate to maintain at least a facade of normality, and had no desire to test the loyalty of the military establishment to the elected government of their country. With coercion ruled out, concessions to Ulster were his only realistic option.

What were these concessions to be? Nationalists were, of course, outraged at any suggestion of partition. Redmond declared it "an abomination and a blasphemy," and his supporters (never mind Sinn Fein and the resurgent IRB) would have great difficulty swallowing any form of partition. Even if the south could be brought to tolerate it, the religious geography of Ulster was extremely messy. Of the nine counties, only Antrim, Down, Derry and Armagh had Protestant majorities, and among these Armagh and Derry were more than 40 percent

Catholic. There were large numbers of Protestants in the other counties, especially Fermanagh and Tyrone, which had Protestant minorities of around 45 percent.

By the time the Home Rule Bill had passed the Commons for the third and final time on May 25, and after much pressure from Asquith, Redmond reluctantly agreed to accept an amending bill with a six-year opt-out for any county that wanted it. This, however, was flatly rejected by Carson as a "sentence of death with a stay of execution for six years," and when the Lords got their hands on this amending bill in July, they belligerently sought to exempt all nine Ulster counties from Home Rule. In the meantime, any doubts as to the intentions of the Ulster Volunteers were firmly dispelled on the night of April 24, 1914, when they brilliantly executed a secret landing of 25,000 German rifles and 3,000,000 rounds of ammunition at Larne, Bangor and Donaghadee. King George V tried to resolve the impasse with a special conference at Buckingham Palace, but this failed. As if tensions were not running high enough already, on July 26, two days after the conference ended, British troops killed three and injured nearly 40 in Dublin. The Irish Volunteers had made their own much smaller and more public landing of arms at Howth, just north of Dublin. The troops sent out to stop them failed, and were harassed and jeered by the crowd on their march back to Dublin. When they reached Bachelor's Walk on the Liffey in the center of Dublin, the troops lost their discipline and fired on the crowd.

All this took place against the backdrop of a Europe drifting ever closer to war, and when Britain declared war on Germany on August 4, 1914, Irish issues were hastily shelved. The Home Rule Bill became law in September but was suspended for either 12 months or until the war ended. Of course no one knew the scale and length of the horror that was to come. Most people thought the war would be a short one and hence assumed that Home Rule would take effect in September 1915. Redmond not only pledged nationalist Ireland to the British war effort, he rashly pledged the Irish Volunteers to the killing fields of Flanders. Given what we know about the horrors of World War I and the Irish War of Independence that followed, this support may seem odd in retrospect, but the vast majority of Irishmen, Unionist and nationalist, supported the war in its early stages. The war was seen as defending "the rights of small nations," notably Catholic Belgium, which had an obvious appealed to moderate Irish nationalists. In addition they hoped that solidarity with Britain and Ulster would not only dispel the Unionist conviction the nationalists were fundamentally disloyal and treacherous, they also thought it stored up a kind of moral credit with the British government which would oblige it to implement Home Rule in full after the war — but then naïvety was the order of the day in 1914. There had been no major European war since the Franco-Prussian War of 1870, which had been short and sharp, and British troops had not fought a properly armed and trained European army since the Crimean War in the 1850s — although the Boers had given them a hard enough time 14 years earlier. In short, very few of the

ABOVE: Sir Edward Carson lends support to a South Londonderry Unionist march. The battle for Home Rule took place against a backdrop of war in Europe in which Irishmen in general — and Ulstermen in particular — played their part.

politicians and soldiers alike knew what they were letting themselves in for. To their credit, the Sinn Fein and IRB leaders immediately denounced Redmond's offer and withdrew from the Irish Volunteers (while keeping the name) with a minority of around 10,000 men. The majority of around 150,000 became the National Volunteers and began joining the British Army in large numbers. The bravery of the Ulstermen who died on the Somme has become the most enduring image of Irish involvement in World War I, but there were thousands of brave Catholic nationalists who joined them, and a number of future IRA men gained their first military experience in the British Army.

Initially the war gave a welcome economic boost to Ireland, especially in the countryside as agricultural prices rose sharply, but as it dragged on "the post-dated cheque" of Home Rule (as MacNeill put it) began to look ever more rubbery. With Unionists such as Carson joining the coalition government of Liberals and Conservatives, and the threat of conscription looming, support for the war waned and a new generation of IRB militant separatists began to gain support for their anti-recruitment campaign. These young activists, led by Patrick Pearse, included Thomas MacDonagh, Sean MacDermott and Joseph Plunkett. They had already

pushed out the older generation of Fenians within the IRB Supreme Council and taken up important positions in the Irish Volunteers. Within weeks of the outbreak of the war, the traditional reaction of Irish separatists kicked in. England's misfortune was, after all, Ireland's opportunity, and they decided very quickly to stage an uprising before war was over.

Those who held such views were a tiny minority in Ireland as a whole, and were only a faction even with the IRB. Most of the Irish Volunteers (including chief of staff Eoin MacNeill, Bulmer Hobson and Michael Rahilly) had little or no idea of their plans. However, the grip of Patrick Pearse and his allies on a range of nationalist organizations increased during 1915. They ousted the non-political Hyde from the Gaelic League and replaced him with the old Fenian Thomas Clarke, who knew a good deal more about dynamite than Gaelic. They also scored a major propaganda coup in hijacking the public funeral of another old Fenian, O'Donovan Rossa. Over his grave Pearse evoked heroes from the past and declared with more truth than he could have guessed:

"Life springs from death; and from the graves of patriot men and women spring living nations. The Defenders of this Realm have worked well in secret and in the open. They think that they have pacified Ireland. They think that they have purchased half of us and intimidated the other half. They think that they have foreseen everything, think that they have provided against everything; but the fools, the fools, the fools — they have left us our Fenian dead, and while Ireland holds these graves, Ireland unfree shall never be at peace."

Within a year Pearse would be lying in his own grave, executed by the British, and would prove a far greater inspiration to nationalists than Rossa.

EASTER 1916

When the rising came on Easter Monday 1916, it surprised almost everyone, not least the British government and army — many of whom were enjoying a sunny day out at the races. The sight of armed men parading in uniform was not uncommon in Dublin, but this time the 1,000 or so men who marched into strategic positions all over Dublin were not on an exercise. Bemused Dubliners gradually realized what was happening when a uniformed man read the Proclamation of the Irish Republic from the steps of the General Post Office on Sackville Street. Having declared "the right of the people of Ireland to the ownership of Ireland, and to the unfettered control of Irish destinies," a poet and schoolmaster called Patrick Pearse went on to outline the nature of this proposed new Irish Republic.

"The Irish Republic is entitled to, and hereby claims, the allegiance of every Irishman and Irishwoman. The Republic guarantees religious and civil liberty, equal rights and equal opportunities to all its citizens, and declares its resolve to pursue the happiness and prosperity of the whole nation . . ."

However, there was more to the Easter Rising than inclusive, non-sectarian, republican liberalism. Behind this rhetoric lay a disturbing and somewhat blasphemous set of ideals. Pearse was undoubtedly an extremely courageous man, who was deeply committed to the welfare of his country and to a vision of a modern, socially just, Gaelic Irish republic. On top of this, he also had a mystical belief in the power of a martyr — often a confused mixture of Christ and Cuchulain — to achieve Irish freedom. Pearse had welcomed the war in Europe for he thought the "red wine" spilt by young men on its battlefields would rejuvenate the world. Bloodshed, for Pearse, was a "cleansing and sanctifying thing." Other leaders of the rising, such as Joseph Plunkett and Thomas MacDonagh, seemed to agree with him, and similar glorifications of sacrifice were not unusual among romantically-inclined nationalists of pre-war Europe. They are, nonetheless, ludicrous. There was certainly nothing very

cleansing about the putrid, mud-filled trenches of France into which thousands of Pearse's countrymen were spilling their "red wine" while Pearse was in the GPO.

More rational nationalists such as MacNeill argued that an uprising with no genuine chance of success was morally repugnant, and once he got wind of the plan he did all in his power as head of the Volunteers to stop it. Volunteer maneuvers had been planned by the IRB Military Council for Easter Sunday (the timing was ideologically significant); they were to be a cover for the rising. But it had no chance of success in the normal sense of the word, especially after the attempt by Sir Roger Casement, a former senior British civil servant, to land 20,000 German rifles in Kerry had failed. The capture of Casement and the ship carrying the guns (called the *Aud*) galvanized MacNeill into calling off the nationwide maneuvers. This left the 1,000 lightly armed volunteers in Dublin (who were later joined by another 600 or so) with no hope of defeating the British Army. In fact the British knew that some sort of rising had been planned, but the capture of the *Aud*, and the cancellation of the Volunteer exercises by MacNeill on the Saturday, convinced them it had been called off.

Among the insurgents were 300 members of Connolly's Irish Citizen Army. Connolly, like many other European socialists during World War I, had been

RIGHT: Roger Casement (top center surrounded by German sailors of submarine U-19) went to Berlin to negotiate for arms for the rising. He returned to Ireland on Good Friday 1916, landing from a U-boat. Arrested on Banna Strand beach by the RIC, he was the last of the insurgents to be executed.

BELOW: Joseph Plunkett, commandant-general of the Irish Republican Army, was executed on May 4, 1916. He was one of the seven signatories of the Proclamation of the Republic delivered from the steps of the GPO at the start of the rising.

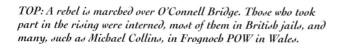

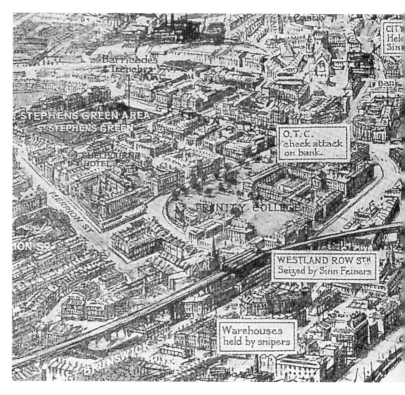

TOP: A rebel is marched over O'Connell Bridge. Those who took part in the rising were interned, most of them in British jails, and many, such as Michael Collins, in Frognoch POW in Wales.

ABOVE: "Holding a Dublin street against the rebels." Most of the 2,500 British troops in Dublin were on leave on Easter Monday, April 24, 1916. There were fewer than 100 men in each of the four main barracks around the city.

ABOVE RIGHT: Damage to Dublin caused by the rising was localized — here is a view of O'Connell Bridge. Note O'Connell's monument at left of picture.

RIGHT: Dublin city center, showing the defensive positions taken by the insurgents during the Easter Rising. Despite these defenses, rifles proved no match for British artillery.

FAR RIGHT: As British soldiers approach the city, they came under heavy fire from de Valera's garrison at Boland's Mills. A detachment of this garrison on the Mount Street Bridge caused by far the heaviest British casualties of the rising.

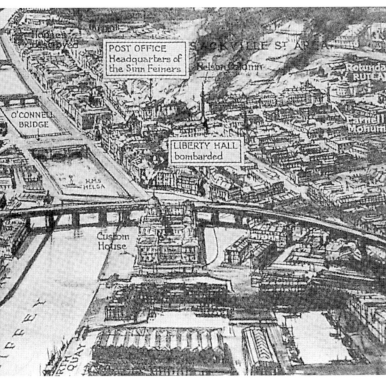

TOP: General Sir John Maxwell, British commander-in-chief during the rising and its aftermath, posing in front of the captured rebel flag, which hangs upside down.

ABOVE CENTER: The burnt out shell of the GPO, the HQ of the insurgents, after the surrender of Pearse to the British forces.

ABOVE: Sackville Street after the fighting.

ABOVE RIGHT: A British Army barricade after the rising.

RIGHT: An armored truck put together quickly — in eight hours! — by British troops in a Dublin engineering yard.

FAR RIGHT: Maxwell was responsible for the execution of the rebels, a policy which was to bring about a change in the people's perception of the insurgents. Yeats' poem, Easter 1916, documents this change in public opinion.

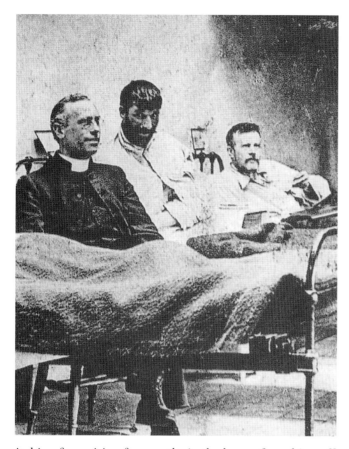

itching for a rising for months in the hope of sparking off a socialist revolution. He had been persuaded to throw in his lot with the IRB despite the fact that he had earlier described Pearse as "a blithering idiot" for his pronouncements on the shedding of blood. That this normally hard-headed, atheistic socialist should join an obviously ill-fated act of messianic martyrdom seems a little odd, but Connolly may have thought they had a real chance of inspiring a national revolution. The fighting lasted for about a week, with the most serious fighting taking place on Mount Street Bridge on the south-eastern approach to the city from the port of Kingstown (now Dun Laoghaire). Around 230 Sherwood Foresters were killed or wounded in the space of six hours by only 17 Volunteers as they tried to fight their way into the city. The commander of this garrison, with its headquarters a few minutes away at Boland's Mills, was one Eamon de Valera.

Many of the strongholds saw little real fighting, although the garrisons at the South Dublin Union Workhouse and around the Four Courts were an exception. The British Army, which contained many Irish troops in Irish regiments, gradually tightened a cordon around the city center. By Friday the GPO was ablaze after a pounding by heavy artillery, and it soon became apparent that more civilians were being killed than combatants. Pearse was genuinely appalled at the carnage, and the decision to surrender once the hopelessness of the situation was obvious reveals a more humane man than his earlier language might suggest. Around 60 Volunteers, 116 soldiers and 16 policemen were killed, but the civilian death toll was nearly 300. In one appalling incident, British troops deliberately shot up North King Street,

ABOVE LEFT: Wounded insurgents in Dublin Castle hospital after the rising.

ABOVE: Patrick Pearse surrenders to General Lowe on April 29, 1916. Faced with his GPO HQ in flames, and in an effort to reduce civilian casualties, he sought terms but was offered only unconditional surrender.

BELOW: Francis Sheehy-Skeffington, a pacifist who took no part in the rising, was one of its most tragic casualties, shot in cold blood by an army officer.

killing a number of innocent residents. Most notoriously, the popular, pacifist, nationalist writer Francis Sheehy-Skeffington, who had taken no part in the rising, was arrested while trying to prevent looting and later shot in cold blood by an army officer. Such incidents caused deep resentment in Ireland, but the rising was not popular at the time. As the captured rebels were led away, they were jeered and spat at by angry Dubliners who were disgusted at the violence and at the smouldering mess they had made of their city. It was the subsequent reaction of the British government which ensured Pearse and his comrades quickly became martyrs for Irish freedom

On May 3, three days after the surrender, Pearse, Clarke and MacDonagh were executed. Over the next nine days another 12 faced a firing squad, finishing with Connolly on May 12; he was shot while seated in a chair because an ankle wound prevented him from standing. Among those executed were all seven signatories of the Proclamation of the Irish Republic, including Joseph Plunkett, Sean MacDermott and Eamonn Ceannt as well as the four already listed.

Given the wartime circumstances, and the fact that the rebels were in open alliance with Germany, the British reaction was predictable and not excessive by the standards of the day. Most of the participants were actually treated with remarkable leniency. The majority of the death sentences were commuted to life imprisonment,

ABOVE: Eamonn Ceannt, another signatory of the Proclamation of the Republic, was also a founding member of the Irish Volunteers and on the Supreme Council of the IRB. He was one of 12 senior figures of the rising executed in Kilmainham Gaol.

BELOW: Eamon de Valera, commander of the garrison at Boland's Mills, surrendered at Broadstone Railway Station on April 30. Sentenced to be executed, this was commuted to life imprisonment because of his American birth.

and in the end future leaders such as Collins and de Valera (whose American birth probably saved him from execution) were only imprisoned for between 8 and 14 months. Many of the younger ones were merely given a stern talking to and told to run on home to their mothers. Indeed, in comparison to the 77 executions carried out by the Free State government on their former colleagues during the Civil War, the British reaction almost seems restrained.

The executions, which took place behind closed doors and under military rather than civil law, touched a nerve in Ireland. Nationalists began to admire the insurgents' courage even if they disagreed with their methods. Almost overnight the attitude to the rising subtly changed. Sir Roger Casement was the last to be executed — hanged in Pentonville Prison in London on August 3 — and by the time the last prisoners returned to Ireland in June 1917 they were being treated like heroes.

THE ROAD TO INDEPENDENCE

As the war dragged on, so the threat of conscription, which had been introduced in Britain in 1916, began to loom over Ireland. Sinn Fein drew on these fears, as well as the anger generated by the executions of 1916, to replace the discredited Irish Parliamentary Party as the voice of Irish nationalism. The Sinn Fein victory of Count Plunkett (Joseph's father) in the Roscommon by-election on February 5, 1917, was the first concrete indication of the change in sentiment. Further by-election victories followed, including that of Eamon de Valera in East Clare shortly after his release from prison in June 1917, and with the death of Thomas Ashe on September 24, separatist sympathies were further stoked. Ashe had been on hunger strike for four days in protest at his arrest for giving an inflammatory speech and had died after being force-fed in prison.

While nationalists hardened their outlook during 1917, Michael Collins was steadily building up an efficient military and intelligence network through the Volunteers and the IRB. The influence of Collins and other veterans of 1916 now became strong within Sinn Fein, but, despite the claims of the government, it had had nothing to do with the rising. As a result of this influx of more militant members, Griffith stood down from the presidency of Sinn Fein in October 1917 in favor of de Valera, who in the following month was also put at the head of the reformed Volunteers. De Valera was the most senior surviving leader of the Easter Rising, which automatically gave him a high standing among separatists, and most saw him as the only figure with enough authority and guile to hold the political and military wings of the "new" Sinn Fein together. Political unity in itself was no mean feat given the very real differences between Griffith's belief in a dual monarchy and passive resistance, and Collins, physical force republicanism — but Sinn Fein's control of the military wing of Irish republicanism was always weak.

The constitution of Sinn Fein was changed to make an independent republic the new goal instead of an Irish parliament under a joint monarch. The exact nature of this future state was deliberately left open to avoid conflict within the party — there would be plenty of time for the Irish people to decide what sort of constitution they wanted once Ireland was free, so the Sinn Fein argument ran. The vagueness of Sinn Fein's program, which allowed supporters to make of it what they wished, was part of its growing appeal. The ascendancy of Sinn Fein was by no means a foregone conclusion, however. In the early spring of 1918 they suffered by-election defeats at the hands of the old Parliamentary Party, and it looked as if their support had peaked. However, in the spring of 1918 two episodes firmly established Sinn Fein's popularity: conscription and the "German Plot" arrests.

The threat of conscription reached a climax in April with the Military Service Act, which allowed the government to introduce conscription whenever it felt necessary. Nationalists of all kinds joined forces in their opposition of the measure, which included a one-day general strike on April 23, and the Parliamentary Party even withdrew from Westminster in protest. Sinn Fein gained most of the credit for the campaign, and the Home Rule Party's withdrawal merely vindicated the Sinn Fein approach. Then, not for the first time, the British government shot itself in the foot with wholesale arrests in May of Sinn Fein leaders on false charges of involvement in a German plot. Collins' intelligence system was good enough at this point to give his colleagues advance warning of the arrests but he was one of the few to take steps to avoid it. In May, de Valera, Griffith and other leaders were sent to prison in England without any evidence at all being produced or charges made.

While all this was happening, the attempts of Prime Minister Lloyd George to find a negotiated solution to the implementation of Home Rule had floundered. Sinn Fein,

RIGHT: The entrance to Kilmainham where the executions of Pearse, Connolly and the other leaders of the rising took place.

ABOVE and BELOW: The return of the heroes — at Christmas 1916 the internees of the rising were given amnesty and returned to a rapturous reception at Kingstown Pier. As Yeats had predicted, "All is changed, changed utterly. A terrible beauty is born."

BELOW LEFT: Constance Georgina Markievicz had married the Polish artist Count Casimir Markievicz and became involved in radical politics. She played a prominent part in helping to relieve distress among the poor of Dublin during the workers' lockout of 1913 and was a founding member of the Irish Citizen Army established at that time. She fought in the College of Surgeons during the rising, was imprisoned in Kilmainham and sentenced to death. The sentence was commuted to life imprisonment because of her sex. In 1918 she became the first woman to be elected to the House of Commons, although she did not take up her seat.

Michael Collins joined the IRB while working in London and returned to Ireland for the rising. Interned in Frongoch until December 1916, he stood for election for Sinn Fein in 1918. Elected to the first Dail Eireann he became Finance Minister. Collins would end the War of Independence by signing the Anglo-Irish Treaty of 1921 and then become commander of the Free State's army in the civil war that followed. He would be ambushed and killed in 1922.

who refused to participate in the Irish Convention chaired by Sir Horace Plunkett, now deemed the degree of independence permitted by the Home Rule Bill to be inadequate, while the Unionists would not budge on the partitioning of a good portion of Ulster. World War I finally ended on November 11, 1918, and within weeks Irish Nationalists had the chance to make their choice between traditional Home Rule and the new Sinn Fein. The result was an overwhelming victory for Sinn Fein with 73 seats to the Irish Parliamentary Party's six. The official and independent Unionists numbered 31, and Sinn Fein's Countess Markievicz became the first woman to be elected to, although not to sit in, the Commons. In terms of overall percentage of the vote, the collapse of the Irish Party was not as dramatic as it looked, and many seats were hard-fought battles. However, the electors had effectively rejected both the concept of Home Rule and the idea that it should be won by activity at Westminster.

Part of the explanation for this seemingly amazing change in voting behavior can be found in the changed electorate of 1918. It was not so much that Sinn Fein won over those who voted for the Home Rule Party last time around (although this certainly happened in some cases) but rather that they won over a new set of voters. About two-thirds of those who voted in 1918 had not voted in the last election of 1910. The impact of a new generation of voters, and the inclusion in the franchise for the first time of women over 30 and all men over 21, worked massively to Sinn Fein's advantage, especially as the party tended to appeal more to the young than the old.

The new Sinn Fein MPs refused to attend Westminster, just as Arthur Griffith had argued that they should many years earlier, and invited all the Irish MPs to join them in a *Dail Eireann* (Irish Assembly). Naturally only the Sinn Fein members attended, and of these only 28 were free to attend, the others being in prison or on the run. The new Dail set up a parallel government, with its own courts and "police force." The Volunteers became, in effect, the army of this new "government" although it was not until August 20 that the Dail demanded the Volunteers' allegiance as the representatives of the Republic. Thereafter they were known as the Irish Republican Army (IRA), but they remained only loosely under the control of the politicians. Michael Collins and, to a lesser extent, Cathal Brugha, who were the Ministers of Finance and of Defence respectively in the new Dail, formed a link between the political and military elements of the Republic, but the IRA often acted without the authorization of the Sinn Fein politicians in the Dail.

The person who did have a measure of control over them, Michael Collins, had seized the initiative among republicans while de Valera was in prison and was determined to force the British government into a confrontation. The Anglo-Irish War is usually said to have begun with the first IRA attack at Soloheadbeg, which killed two policemen (symbolically, this took place on January 21, 1919, on the same day as the first meeting of the Dail) but as 1919 progressed Ireland only gradually drifted into serious conflict. The path of violence was neither inevitable nor unanimously supported within Sinn Fein, and the most intense violence occurred between spring 1920 and the truce of July 9, 1921. In 1919, many in Sinn Fein pinned their hopes on the admission of Irish representatives to the World War I peace negotiations at Versailles and international (especially American) pressure on the British government.

On April 1, 1919, the Dail elected de Valera (who had escaped from Lincoln prison on February 3) as its president, but two months later he left for America where he spent the next year and a half. His lengthy absence at such a crucial time on a fund-raising and propaganda tour can only be understood in terms of the importance placed on American recognition of Irish independence during this period. In this respect de Valera failed. Despite President Wilson's faith in self-determination, he had no desire to tread on British toes in what he knew they regarded as an internal issue (Wilson's Ulster Protestant ancestry may also be relevant here). However, de Valera's trip was successful in raising precious funds for the fledgling government (over $5 million), despite his clashes with longstanding Irish-American leaders John Devoy and Judge Daniel Cohalan.

While de Valera was away the influence of Collins grew ever stronger, as he combined his role as Minister of Finance with the presidency of the IRB and de facto control of the IRA. Collins, who was born in Co. Cork in 1890, had worked in London as a Post Office clerk before returning to Ireland to fight in the 1916 rising. A member of the Gaelic League as well as the IRB, Collins effectively began his career as Ireland's most impressive military organizer in the prison camps of Frongoch in North Wales, where he established many contacts during his internment in 1916. By 1920 he was directing an efficient and ruthless campaign of assassinations and ambushes on the British forces. The Royal Irish Constabulary, most of whom were Catholic and Irish, bore the brunt of the IRA's efforts, with around 400 being killed during the war. After January 1920, the notorious "Black and Tans" and "Auxies" (Auxiliaries) increasingly replaced the demoralized and depleted RIC. Both of these forces were technically under the direction of the RIC, because the British government was reluctant to give the struggle the

BELOW: The Auxiliaries. Together with the Black and Tans — also demobbed World War I veterans — they fought a savage war against the IRA in 1920–21 and tended to replace the depleted and demoralized Royal Irish Constabulary.

status of a genuine war, and sought to pass it off as a problem of civil order. Nevertheless, both units operated more like military than civilian bodies.

The Black and Tans, so-called because their uniforms were a mixture of army khaki and police black, were recruited from unemployed ex-soldiers from the ranks. The Auxiliaries, so-called because they were officially auxiliary members of the RIC, were all ex-army officers. Both tended to be tough, experienced soldiers who had seen action in World War I, and the relatively high rates of pay (10 shillings and £1 a day respectively) were a big incentive for many. A vicious cycle of assassination or ambush by the IRA followed by brutal and indiscriminate reprisals by the Black and Tans (this label often covered Auxiliaries as well in popular usage) developed during 1920. The most famous example was the "Bloody Sunday" episode of November 21, 1920. In retaliation for the assassination by Collins' men of 14 undercover British intelligence agents, the Black and Tans opened fire on the crowd at a Gaelic Football match in Croke Park, killing 12 and injuring scores. There were many other similar incidents as "official" reprisals were carried out in a completely indiscriminate manner on any local populace

RIGHT: The Illustrated London News for Saturday, December 18, 1920, shows the devastation after the burning of Cork by the Black and Tans.

BELOW: Croke Park Stadium, which saw the Black and Tans kill 12 of the crowd at a Gaelic Football match on the infamous "Bloody Sunday."

FAR RIGHT: The Illustrated London News reported, "The worst act of Sinn Fein arson: the burning of the Customs House at Dublin, on May 25, 1921 . . . The photograph was taken while the fire was in progress, and before the dome melted."

THE BURNING OF CORK : DEVASTATION IN THE HEART OF THE CITY AFTER A NIGHT OF FIRE.

which was suspected of supporting IRA attacks. The shooting up and burning of Cork city center by Black and Tans on the night of December 11 was a particularly notorious incident, and it became common for Sinn Fein members and suspected IRA men to be dragged from their beds in the middle of the night, to be beaten, imprisoned and even murdered.

The IRA, of course, also contributed heavily to the general frightfulness of this era. As well as the shootings, arson attacks and the like, they intimidated and often murdered anyone whose activities could be interpreted as supporting the British administration. This went much further than policemen and soldiers, and could include laborers who simply worked for the government. Both sides committed appalling atrocities which shocked and sickened not only people in Ireland, but in the US and Britain as well. During 1921 pressure mounted for a political settlement. The IRA knew that, despite its remarkable success in making Ireland ungovernable, it could never defeat the massively superior British forces. The British government knew it could not defeat the IRA quickly and that public opinion in Britain would not tolerate the current levels of violence indefinitely.

Despite the obvious logic of the situation, when the war ended quite suddenly with a truce on July 9, 1921, it took many by surprise. Negotiations began on October 11 with Lloyd George, Winston Churchill and Lord Birkenhead leading the British side, and Collins, Griffith and Kevin O'Higgins heading the Irish delegation. Crucially, de Valera did not attend the negotiations. This was a mistake which led to a tragic misunderstanding of the precise role and authority of Irish delegation. Collins and Griffith regarded themselves as plenipotentiaries with full powers to make agreements on Ireland's behalf. De Valera assumed that any treaty would be referred back to himself and the rest of the Sinn Fein cabinet before it was signed. On December 6 the Anglo-Irish Treaty was signed after a night of intense negotiations and without referring the terms back to Dublin. It became one of the most controversial documents in Irish history.

Much has been made of the ultimatum given to the Irish delegation on the last night of negotiations by Lloyd George. In a staggering piece of brinksmanship he demanded they sign that evening or face a resumption of war in three days. In retrospect it seems amazing that Collins and Griffith allowed Lloyd George to get away with this without even insisting on a phone call to de

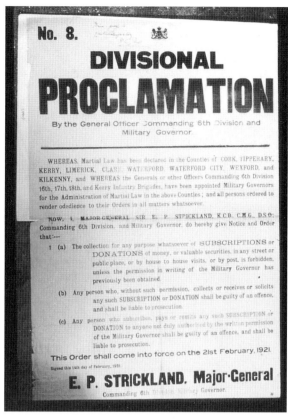

Valera, but the substance of the deal was not unfavorable to Ireland, given both sides' initial starting positions. The nub of the issue at the time was the extent and nature of the connection between the two countries. The Irish wanted a fully independent republic, while the British were prepared to offer dominion status within the empire similar to that of Canada. What they got was an Irish "Free State" with complete control of internal legislation, finances and defense (although the British were to retain a number of naval bases). It was, as Collins rightly put it, "the freedom to achieve freedom." De Valera knew that compromise was necessary and, in retrospect, his ingenious proposal of "external association" with Britain in his Document No. 2 does not look all that different to the actual treaty, but there was one crucial difference: it avoided an explicit oath of allegiance to the British crown. It was this last point that particularly stuck in proud republican throats — which had already declared their allegiance to "the Republic."

The most surprising aspect of the arguments for and against the treaty, given later events, was the relative unimportance of partition. In many respects, partition was already a foregone conclusion, though few wished to believe it in the south. Back in December 1920, the Government of Ireland Act had already established two separate parliaments: one for the six Ulster counties of Antrim, Armagh, Down, Fermanagh, Derry and Tyrone, and one for the rest of Ireland. Sinn Fein ignored the new parliament in Dublin, which immediately became dead in the water, but the Ulster Unionists embraced the Belfast parliament and effectively ensured Ireland's partition while the Anglo-Irish War was still in full swing — nearly a year before the Anglo-Irish Treaty was signed. Many in both Ireland and Britain still thought partition would be temporary, and the promise of the Boundary Commission to reassess the border along religious lines bolstered the Irish delegation's hopes that Ireland could soon be reunited — especially when accompanied by hints from Lloyd George that it would recommend such large transfers of territory from the north to the south as to make the north unviable on its own. However the vague conditions for the setting up of the Boundary Commission are striking and show a Sinn Fein failure to appreciate the tenacity of Ulster Unionism.

After a lengthy and emotional debate in the Dail, the treaty was approved by the dangerously narrow margin of 64 to 57 on January 7, 1922. This was not acceptable

ABOVE: *The Four Courts building was designed by James Gandon (as was the Customs House). It was occupied by the anti-treaty forces and gutted during an assault by Free State troop. This action began the Irish Civil War as well as destroying the neighboring Public Records Office with its collection of documents dating back to the 13th century. This is a 1940s' view of the Four Courts over the Liffey.*

ABOVE LEFT: *"Divisional proclamation by the General Officer Commanding 6th Division and Military Governor"; proclamation of Maj-Gen Strickland prohibiting the collection of subscriptions or donations in the south or south-east; February 14, 1921.*

BELOW: *The Sinn Fein delegation to the treaty negotiations of 1921. Seated (center) at the table is Michael Collins. On the left edge of the picture (and almost cropped out) is Arthur Griffith and seated on the right is Robert Barton. These three Dail ministers headed the delegation. Erskine Childers is standing at the rear.*

to hard-line republicans such as Cathal Brugha and Austin Stack, as well as de Valera himself; they refused to recognize the new state's legitimacy, and the latter stood down from the presidency.

CIVIL WAR 1922

The Civil War between the pro- and anti-treaty IRA was not only more scarring and vicious than the War of Independence, it shaped the future course of Irish politics right down to the present. There was, naturally, a reluctance on both sides to initiate full-scale conflict with former friends and comrades, but once hostilities began in earnest, the tactics of both sides became merciless. Political principles and personal honor were, of course, vital factors, but personal animosities also played an important part in the taking of sides. Cathal Brugha and Collins, for example, had often clashed in their attempts to control the IRA, but most important was the rivalry between Collins and de Valera. On the face of it, before the truce, de Valera as the wily and flexible politician should have been on the pro-treaty side, while Collins, the ruthless and committed physical force republican, seems a more likely candidate for hard-line opposition to a compromise with the British. Yet Collins turned out a pragmatist and de Valera an obstinate ally of extremist republicans. In practice de Valera exercised little control over the formidable military leaders of the anti-treaty IRA, which included Liam Lynch, Liam Mellows, Oscar Traynor, Ernie O'Malley and Rory O'Connor. As a former president of the Dail, he gave their struggle some degree of democratic legitimacy, and he was instrumental in arranging the final abandonment of the struggle by the defeated anti-treaty forces.

At a lower level, the decisions of individual commanders often decided the allegiances of their men, and so in early 1922 the picture was incredibly confused as rival units took up positions in close proximity to each other. Further complications arose from the Free State's support for both pro- and anti-treaty IRA units who were defending Catholics from the appalling sectarian violence which had flared up in Ulster. Between January and June, 93 Protestants and 171 Catholics were killed in the six counties, while a draconian and frankly bigoted Unionist government sought to impose its own variety of order. The Special Powers Act, and the all-Protestant A- and B-Special forces set up to enforce it, set the northern state in an aggressively Protestant mode from the start. Meanwhile, in the south, British Army Barracks were taken over by both sides, and the Irregulars (as the anti-treaty forces came to be known) took up positions in Gandon's magnificent 18th century Four Courts building on the Liffey.

A last-ditch attempt to avoid conflict was made in May

DAN BREEN'S APPEAL

D.BREEN'S APPEAL TO HIS OLD COMRADES NOW IN THE FREE STATE ARMY.

Comrades,

ARE YOU AWARE that you are fighting against the Republic that you fought to establish in 1916, and that was maintained and is going to be maintained?

ARE YOU AWARE that England tried to disestablish the Republic through a reign of Black and Tan terror?

ARE YOU AWARE that she is now using the so-called Provisional Government to try where she failed?

ARE YOU AWARE that YOU are the Black and Tans of to-day, the only difference is the uniform?

ARE YOU AWARE that the death of CATHAL BRUGHA is a damnable and eternal stain on the uniform?

ARE YOU AWARE that CATHAL BRUGHA died as my comrade, SEAN TREACY, died?-- no surrender to enemies of the Republic was their cry.

ARE YOU AWARE that there are hundreds of MEN who will die as Brugha and Treacy died in defence of the Republic?

ARE YOU AWARE that I did my best to maintain the army for the Republic, but I failed because your section took orders from our only enemy--England?

Comrades, I thought my term of soldiering was over, but duty again called me to defend the Republic, which I will do or die in the attempt. Will you again stand with me as my comrades in arms, or will you continue to fight with England against me?

Dan Breen.

with a somewhat undemocratic Collins-de Valera pact before the June 1922 general election. Pro- and anti-treaty Sinn Fein candidates would not oppose each other, but rather stand as a panel of agreed candidates reflecting the pre-election strength of the factions in the Dail. But co-operation did not last long, and the results of the election demonstrated that the 26 counties backed pro-treaty candidates by a healthy majority. Indeed the Labour party (reflecting the serious industrial and agrarian unrest of this period) received more votes than anti-treaty Sinn Fein candidates — who received only 134,000 out of the 620,000 votes cast. Interestingly, more votes were cast for socialists, farmers' parties and other independents than either wing of Sinn Fein. As these were all basically pro-treaty, and the pro-treaty Sinn Fein candidates themselves polled 239,000 votes, the result was effectively an endorsement of the Free State. De Valera arrogantly claimed that he only had to look into his own heart to know the true feelings of the Irish people concerning the treaty, but the ballot box told a different story.

Having been backed by a popular mandate for the treaty, Collins and Griffith came under pressure from the British to take action against the Irregulars, who were thought to be responsible for the assassination of Field Marshal Sir Henry Wilson — the former Chief of Imperial Staff and recently appointed security advisor to the Northern Ireland government. (Ironically, it was probably Collins himself who had ordered the assassination.) Collins' decision to stop support for the IRA in the north also contributed to growing tensions, but the audacious capture by the Irregulars of General "Ginger" O'Connell, the Deputy Chief of Staff of the Free State Army, was the final straw. On June 28, 1922, Free State troops began shelling the Four Courts (using artillery borrowed from the British) after an ultimatum to withdraw was ignored. The Civil War had begun.

The stronghold of the Irregulars was in the "Munster Republic" of the south and west. Roughly speaking, they tried to hold a line from Waterford to Limerick, but both of these were captured by Free State forces by the end of July. The Irregulars were then pushed back through Tipperary into their strongholds of Cork, Kerry and parts of Limerick. After successful assaults by sea on north Kerry and Cork, the Free State Army was able to establish itself in the Irregulars' rear, and although the ambushes and assassinations continued until May 1923, by the end of August 1922 the contest was not in doubt.

Despite this military success, August 1922 was a black month for the Irish Free State. Within the space of 11 days Griffith had died from a cerebral haemorrhage and Collins was shot dead in an ambush at Bealnablath in his home county of Cork. William Cosgrave (as the new head

LEFT: "Dan Breen's Appeal": a printed notice signed "Dan Breen," published late 1922, urges his former comrades to join him "to defend the Republic, which I will do or die in the attempt."

ABOVE: "Halligan's Bread" — a scene in Dublin during the Civil War.

BELOW: The city streets of Ireland were often the front line during the War of Independence and the Civil War. Here a Crossley armored car fires on smoking building. These vehicles were used by both the British and Free State forces.

of the provisional government) took up the reins of power and with the able assistance of Kevin O'Higgins prosecuted the war with vigor and severity. Between November 1922 and the end of the war, 77 Irregulars were shot under emergency powers which included an automatic death sentence for the possession of arms: one of those executed was Erskine Childers, who was caught in possession of a pearl-handled revolver given to him by Collins himself. Among the others executed were Liam Mellows and Rory O'Connor, while Cathal Brugha and Liam Lynch fell in the fighting itself. The violent deaths of so many heroes from 1916 and the war of independence left deep and lasting scars on the fledgling state.

THE FREEDOM TO ACHIEVE FREEDOM

The decade after the Civil War was characterized by the sober, conservative, constitutional government of Cumann na nGaedheal. This new pro-treaty party, with Cosgrave, as President of the Excutive Council and O'Higgins as Minister for Home Affairs, set about the task of restoring order and stability in difficult circumstances. Between 1923 and 1927 the Irish Free State could hardly be said to have operated as a normal democracy. The political supporters of the Civil War republicans,

still known as Sinn Fein and with de Valera as their leader, refused to take the oath of allegiance to George V and hence their seats in the Dail — despite winning 44 seats (or 30 percent of the vote) in the 1923 election. Hence, with the exception of the relatively small Labour Party, there was no proper parliamentary opposition during these years.

Furthermore, although the IRA had largely gone underground and had little public support, it maintained a low level campaign. This took the form of destroying symbols of the British connection as well as the occasional attack on the new police force, the *Garda Siochana* or "Civic Guard." Such attacks prompted a stern response from the government, especially after the murder in 1927 of the IRA's bête noire, Kevin O'Higgins, by rogue elements of that organization. The Public Safety Act soon followed, which gave strong powers to the government in its attempt to suppress the IRA. Thankfully, after the election of that year, de Valera and his new party *Fianna Fail* (Warriors of Ireland), decided to enter the Dail. They refused to take the oath verbally, but signed their names in a register which was deemed to amount to the same thing. They were, in the memorable words of Sean Lemass, still only "a slightly constitutional party," but

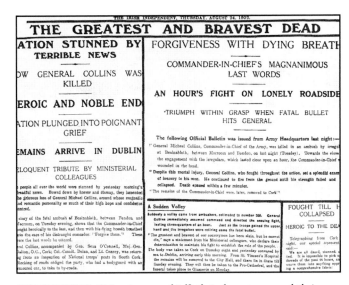

THE IRISH INDEPENDENT, THURSDAY, AUGUST 24, 1922.

THE GREATEST AND BRAVEST DEAD

ATION STUNNED BY TERRIBLE NEWS

W GENERAL COLLINS WAS KILLED

EROIC AND NOBLE END

ATION PLUNGED INTO POIGNANT GRIEF

EMAINS ARRIVE IN DUBLIN

ELOQUENT TRIBUTE BY MINISTERIAL COLLEAGUES

FORGIVENESS WITH DYING BREATH

COMMANDER-IN-CHIEF'S MAGNANIMOUS LAST WORDS

AN HOUR'S FIGHT ON LONELY ROADSIDE

·TRIUMPH WITHIN GRASP WHEN FATAL BULLET HITS GENERAL

PORTRAIT OF THE LATE GEN. COLLINS

BELOW LEFT: IRA prisoners shield their faces to conceal their identities.

ABOVE and RIGHT: The Irish Independent of August 24, 1922, reports the death of Michael Collins. Founded in 1891, the newspaper was taken over by William Murphy in 1905: it supported the treaty and in the 1920s and 1930s was generally identified with Cumann na nGaedheal and Fine Gael.

they had decided to pursue their republican goals democratically and peacefully. The participation in the Dail of their 44 members (which was only three fewer than Cumann na nGaedheal) was vital to the stability of the still fragile state.

The partition of the north was still a pressing concern for most Catholic Irishmen, but after the disorder and chaos of the Civil War, Ulster Unionists were even less likely to want to join the south. The Boundary Commission finally began its work on November 6, 1924, but it gradually became clear that it was not going to recommend radical changes to the border. There were significant areas of Tyrone, Fermanagh, south Armagh and south Down which should have been passed back to the south because of their Catholic majorities, but the South African judge appointed by the British government to chair the commission, Richard Feetham, took the controversial view that the political and economic stability of Northern Ireland should come before local preferences.

Much of the blame for this state of affairs must be attributed to the original Irish treaty delegation for its failure to define precisely the criteria that would be used by the Boundary Commission, but it is doubtful if significant parts of the six counties could have been wrested from the Ulster Unionists in 1925 without serious bloodshed. Professor Eoin MacNeill, one of the original founders of both the Irish Volunteers and the Gaelic League, headed the Irish negotiators on the Boundary Commission, but he had little chance of altering its findings in the face of combined British and Northern Irish opposition, and he resigned before its findings could be published. The Free State government now faced the dangerous prospect of a legally binding report finalized purely by the British and Northern Ireland delegation (which could have transferred a mainly Protestant por-

tion of Donegal to the north). As a result, in December 1925, Cosgrave agreed to maintain the border as it was, in return for Ireland's release from its liability for a portion of the British National debt, as agreed in the treaty. Republicans were predictably loud in their criticism of the deal.

By the early 1930s, economic problems and the boredom that afflicts all longstanding democratic governments began to take their toll on support for Cumann na nGaedheal. The establishment of the Agricultural Credit Corporation (1927), the Electricity Supply Board (1927), and especially the Shannon Hydro-Electric Scheme (1929) were all beneficial reforms, but endemic poverty and poor economic growth were not seriously tackled. Hence, in the 1932 elections de Valera's Fianna Fail became the largest single party and with the help of the Labour Party formed a new government. It is a testimony to the democratic ideals and professional integrity of the Free State civil service and military that the handover of power to their erstwhile civil war enemies went so smoothly.

De Valera gradually set about dismantling, the most offensive parts of the treaty. He began by withholding the land annuities which were still being paid to the British government for the purchase of land before independence. This prompted an "Economic War" with Britain which Ireland was ill-placed to wage. Protective tariffs kept out British goods, and agricultural prices (especially that of cattle) slumped as embargoes were placed on Irish exports to Britain. As in the rest of Europe, economic depression created unstable conditions. With the IRA resurgent under a more sympathetic government, a group of ex-Free State army members created their own rival organization. The Army Comrades Association (later renamed the National Guard) was founded to protect ex-

PUT AN END TO IRELAND'S NIGHTMARE.

BREAK THE CONNECTION WITH ENGLAND.

1925

FREE STATE MINISTER HOGAN SAYS :— "We'll bloody well execute again."
FREE STATE MINISTER O'HIGGINS SAYS :— "77 Executions, and 777 more if necessary."
AND THE NEW COERCION ACT IS DESIGNED TO MAKE THEM "NECESSARY."

ON'T HELP TO FORGE A NEW LINK TO THE CHAIN BY VOTI
FREE STATE.
OTE REPUBLICAN—AND GIVE IRELAND A CHANC

LEFT: "Put an end to Ireland's nightmare: break the connection with England"; a republican election poster for the 1927 election. It lists a fanciful representation of executions through the centuries up to 1925.

RIGHT: Ireland's greatest poet became a Senator of the Irish Free State. W. B. Yeats is pictured here in 1930.

stitution was approved by the Dail and on July 1 by 57 percent of those voted in a referendum. This constitution represented a mixture of liberal democracy and Catholic social teaching, the latter guaranteeing further northern alienation from the ethos of the southern state. Talks followed with Britain which secured British withdrawal from the ports still occupied since the treaty and, by the outbreak of World War II, de Valera was in a position to maintain Irish neutrality despite the lingering connections with Britain.

This gradual change in Ireland's constitutional status had actually begun with Cosgrave's government. Membership of the League of Nations in 1923, and the announcement in 1929 that international disputes involving Ireland would be dealt with by the Court of International Justice, were both indications of independent statehood rather than Commonwealth status. The first significant change in Anglo-Irish relations after the treaty was de Valera's 1937 constitution. Notable features of the new constitution were the introduction of proportional representation, the creation of a president as formal head of state to replace the governor-general and a new senate (with more limited powers) based on corporate and vocational membership rather than election. Significantly there was no mention of either the King or the Commonwealth, and the crown became merely a symbol of co-operation. Still de Valera did not yet feel strong enough formally to reject the treaty, and so there is no mention of a republic either. The most important features were probably the territorial claim to "the whole island of Ireland" in Article 2 and the "special position" given to the Catholic Church in Article 44. The latter did guarantee freedom of conscience and worship, but any constitution which banned divorce and began by invoking the authority of "the Most Holy Trinity" was hardly likely to encourage Ulster Protestants to put themselves under its protection. Similarly the claim of sovereignty over Northern Ireland in Article 2 was to prove a long standing obstacle to good relations with that state.

The Economic War was ended in 1938 by a highly favorable series of agreements with the British. As well as the reversion of the treaty ports, the outstanding annuities were reduced from over £100 million to £10 million. Furthermore, Irish agricultural products were allowed back into Britain largely tariff-free, while Ireland could retain some of its protective tariffs for her fledgling industries.

As de Valera moved steadily closer to a republic, his relations with the hard-line republicans in the IRA actually worsened. They reached a crisis point when bomb attacks in both Eire (as it was now called) and England led to a renewed clampdown and the Offences Against

government figures and supporters from IRA intimidation, but they soon took on some of the characteristics of Italian fascism. Popularly known as "the Blueshirts" for their attire, they adopted a mixture of Catholic social conservatism and authoritarian corporatism, but were never as vicious or as racist as other European Fascists. They were commanded by an ex-IRA and Free State general, Eoin O'Duffy, who had been dismissed from his post as chief of the Garda by the incoming Fianna Fail Government for his rigorous application of Cosgrave's anti-IRA legislation. O'Duffy's eccentricities, and clashes between the Blueshirts and the IRA, soon reflected badly on the former party of government, who had re-emerged in 1934 as Fine Gael. In September 1934 O'Duffy was forced to resign, but the damage had been done, and Fine Gael would not recover fully until after World War II.

As the 1930s wore on, the uneasy accommodation between de Valera and the IRA came under strain. By giving ex-IRA Irregulars pensions in 1934, and offering many jobs in the army and the police force, de Valera had gained tenuous IRA support. However, he was determined not to become a hostage to their aims and after increasing tension, the IRA was declared illegal in 1936. In December 1936, de Valera used the abdication of Edward VIII as an opportunity to pass an amending act which removed all reference to the crown and the governor-general. By June of the following year his new con-

the State Act in 1939. After a major raid on an army weapons depot in Phoenix Park, two further emergency bills against the IRA were passed in January 1940.

This pointless IRA campaign was soon dwarfed by the outbreak of World War II on September 1, 1939. De Valera immediately declared Ireland's neutrality despite considerable pressure not only from Britain, but from America also. The use of Irish ports and airfields would have extended the cover available to the vital Atlantic convoys by several hundred miles, which would have undoubtedly saved the lives of thousands of Allied seamen as well as thousands of tons of supplies. Yet, in retrospect, it is not hard to understand why a small and relatively poor country, so often ill-served by Britain in the past, was reluctant to throw in its lot with that country and risk whatever fragile wealth and stability it had managed to achieve since 1921. The Irish government was naturally more sympathetic to the Allies than to the Germans, especially once the true nature of Nazi activities became apparent, but the formalities of neutrality were strictly observed right up until the end — even to the point of de Valera paying a formal visit to the German Ambassador in Dublin to pass on his condolences on the death of Hitler in 1945. Such actions outraged Churchill, who was tempted to take forcible possession of southern Irish ports. The use of Northern Ireland as a British and American base was a partial compensation for the Allies, but even this prompted a formal protest from de Valera when American troops arrived in 1942. Within Ireland, however, neutrality was certainly popular and de Valera's principled stance admired, although as in World War I, many Irishmen from north and south volunteered to fight in the British armed forces. Eire suffered shortages, economic stagnation and even a few bombing raids, but neutrality saved it from the full horrors of war. Perhaps more importantly, it gave the clearest proof that Eire was effectively an independent sovereign republic.

Of course Northern Ireland's status ensured that it played an important part in the war effort, and as such it was bombed heavily in 1940 and 1941. This divergence in wartime experience between north and south, served to separate their sympathies even further. Since the Boundary Commission had failed to revise the border in 1925, the initial Catholic boycott of the northern state was reluctantly dropped as the full horror of a potentially permanent partition dawned on Catholics. Nationalist representatives began taking their seats in the Northern Ireland Parliament (which after 1932 was housed in a grand new building at Stormont) but it was hardly a stable situation, with around a third of the population desiring the state's destruction. An intransigent Protestant mentality pervaded its outlook and institutions. Sir James Craig, its first Prime Minister, openly declared Northern Ireland a Protestant state with a Protestant Parliament and boasted of being an Orangeman first and a politician second. His successor in 1940, Sir Basil Brooke, carried a similar mentality right down to the 1960s, and the gerrymandering of electoral boundaries, which secured Protestant majorities even on those councils where Catholics should have had a majority (most notoriously in

the city of Londonderry) backed up Craig's claim. All this insecurity favored a conservative outlook which meant that serious social problems in the six counties were neglected. Poverty, bad housing, poor public health and chronic unemployment were problems throughout Ulster, but systematic discrimination meant that Catholics got the worst of a bad lot.

When the war in Europe ended in May 1945, Churchill's victory radio address praised the north and criticized Irish neutrality. He argued that the British had shown "a restraint and poise with which . . . history will find few parallels" by not laying a violent hand on Ireland, even though "at times it would have been quite easy and quite natural." Such a cavalier attitude to Irish sovereignty, whatever the circumstances, could not go unchallenged. A few days later a composed de Valera gave his famous and dignified response to Churchill. Rather than treating Churchill's remarks as British arrogance, he gently pointed out the danger of making the needs of large states into moral codes irrespective of the rights of their smaller neighbors. He praised Britain for its self-restraint and even attributed Churchill's comments to the excitement of victory. Such a statesmanlike and restrained response was a symbolic coming of age for the new state — a shift in attitude from rebellious republicanism to independent statehood. It gained de Valera a standing ovation in the Dail.

By the general election 1948, de Valera had been in power for nearly 16 years and, despite his wartime popularity, voters were ready for a change. A new coalition government, headed by John Costello of Fine Gael, came to power. It relied on the support of an assortment of independent parties, including a radical, new, leftist, republican party called *Clann na Poblachta* (Children of the Republic). The latter injected some much needed youth and social concern into the tired politics of Eire. Conservative attitudes to housing, health and welfare had left the Irish poor occupying many of the same slums as they had before independence — and in not much better health. Rates of tuberculosis and child mortality were particularly high for a western country. The role of the church could also be oppressive, with censorship much more intrusive than in Britain or the USA. The constitution of 1937 had established the need for freedom of expression to be compatible with morality (in other words Catholic morality) and social order. Many of the tensions between old and new Ireland were to come to a head in 1951 with the resignation of the brilliant young Clann na Plobochta Heath minister Noel Browne in response to Church interference in his much-needed health reforms, but this is beyond our period.

Ironically, it was the Fine Gael government, a political descendant of the first Free State government, that finally brought about an Irish Republic and not de Valera. The Republic of Ireland Act was announced almost casually by Costello while in Canada and came into effect on 21 December 1948. On 18 April 1949, Eire became the Republic of Ireland and left the Commonwealth. The destiny of the 26 counties of the south was now firmly in their own hands.

RIGHT: *Eamon de Valera bestrode Irish politics like a colossus: from the Easter Rising, when he was lucky not to be executed, through his time as leader, to the end of World War II and eventual defeat at the polls in 1948. De Valera returned as Taoiseach for two further terms of office in the 1950s, finally ending his active political career in 1959 when he became president. The bottom picture shows him in July 1919; the top shows him and his cabinet following the 1933 General Election.*

THE UNITED STATES CONNECTION

ABOVE and RIGHT: Often the last view of the Old World for emigrants would be the skyline of Liverpool. The prize was the New World, as epitomized by the Statue of Liberty, although often this meant exchanging the dire conditions of the famine for insanitary tenements in one of the US's growing cities.

PREVIOUS PAGE: Named after its 18th century owner Sam Ellis, Ellis Island was used as a fort and arsenal; from 1892 until 1943, however, it served as entry point for immigrants to the United States.

The famous exhortation of America to the Old World to "give me your tired, your poor, your huddled masses yearning to breathe free" could have been written for Irish immigrants alone. Of the 35 or so million emigrants to America between 1800 and 1921, over seven million (or 20 percent) came from Ireland, and many of them were indeed, tired and poor. The enduring image of this mass migration is of the famine-era coffin ships unloading their diseased and starving cargo onto American shores only to be crammed into the insanitary tenements of Boston and New York. From there the strong and resourceful struggled towards modest, or occasionally spectacular, success in this burgeoning new nation, while the weak and unfortunate fell by the wayside. For many Irish emigrants, this was indeed the pattern, but such images reflect only part of the Irish-American story.

Irishmen and women had been leaving their homeland in search of more prosperous and less oppressive lives since the 17th century — the most famous exodus being that of the Catholic military elite leaving for service in the armies of the French, Spain and the Austrian Empire. Numerically this movement was quite small, but on a larger scale, Irish emigrants, and especially Ulster Presbyterians, had been settling in colonial America since the early 18th century. These rugged, God-fearing people frequently settled in Virginia and Pennsylvania and were often the most successful pioneers in the Appalachians. Their independent-minded religion and vigorous anti-English sentiments also put them at the forefront of revolutionary opposition to British rule. From this Ulster stock came eight of the signatories of the Declaration of Independence (there was only one Catholic Irish-American, Charles Carroll), as did Presidents Andrew Jackson, James Knox Polk, James Buchanan, Chester Alan Arthur and Woodrow Wilson. There had been Catholics, and Irish Catholics, in America since the founding of Maryland as a haven for English Catholics in the 17th century, but their numbers were relatively small.

United Irish radical exiles from the 1798 rebellion, both Protestant and Catholic, added color and vigor to American politics, usually as Jeffersonian democrats, while some, such as Thomas Addis Emmet (older brother of Robert) and William James MacNeven, became leading citizens in New York. Their numbers were not large and in the early 19th century there was no recognizable urban, Catholic, Irish-American. Communities of Catholic and Protestant Irish were scattered. They mixed fairly freely and were as likely to be in the country or in the south as in the northern cities. This would change in the 19th century.

The large-scale Catholic Irish emigration to America did not begin with the famine: there had been significant growth in Catholic Irish immigration in the 1820s and up to 40,000 people a year were arriving during the 1830s. Around this time the descendants of the Ulster Protestants began calling themselves "Scots-Irish" to distinguish their beliefs and characters from the more recent

Caricatures of the Irish emigrant before and after emigration, as published by Sala at Berlin in the late 19th century — LEFT "Outward-Bound (Dublin)," a badly dressed emigrant reads a poster advertising passage to New York. RIGHT "Homeward-bound (New York)," a well-dressed emigrant reads a poster advertising passage to Dublin.

Catholic emigrants. Henceforth, and perhaps unfortunately for the future of Catholic-Protestant relations back in Ireland, the new Catholic emigrants had a monopoly on the label "Irish." By the eve of the famine these Irish Catholics had already established large communities in New York, Boston and Philadelphia, and the trend would have continued even if that catastrophe had not occurred. The scale of the impetus given to Irish America by the famine was nonetheless enormous. It can be best summed up in the estimate that, of the two million or so who emigrated between 1845 and 1855, only about half would have gone anyway. This would still have had a significant impact on America, although the epic and traumatic quality of the migration would obviously have been lessened.

From this point on, emigration became a constant, if much lamented, feature of Irish life up to the mid-20th century and beyond. There were many destinations. Large numbers settled in Britain, itself an expanding and wealthy country throughout this period and a greater industrial power than America until the 1890s. Emigration to Britain also had the advantage of an easier return to Ireland, but historical and political attitudes in both countries made it less appealing for most than a fresh start in a new country. Significant numbers made the long sea voyage to South Africa and more made the even longer journey to Australia and New Zealand, while Canada appealed increasingly to many Protestant emigrants. Nevertheless, in most years, over 80 percent of Irish emigrants went to the US. Attracted by the higher wages (often up to three times those in Ireland), the seemingly limitless industrial expansion, and the freedom they expected to find there, America was undoubtedly the nation of choice for Irish emigrants. There were, however, significant oscillations in rates of emigration, which were closely related to economic conditions in both Ireland and America, as well as war in Europe.

After the famine peak years of 1846 to 1852, when between 200,000 and 250,000 left each year, gradual economic recovery in Ireland reduced the annual flow to around 50,000 in the late 1850s. This climbed steeply again to around 100,000 per year in the early 1860s (the Civil War seemingly proving no disincentive), before plummeting to around 20,000 each year during the mid-1870s due to severe economic recession in America (and elsewhere). However the agricultural crisis of the Land War years (1879–83) soon sent totals back to 1860s' levels. Thereafter emigration, while remaining high, declined steadily until the outbreak of World War I in 1914 once more stemmed the flow. This was partly due to a booming wartime Irish agricultural economy, and partly to the

ABOVE: Conditions on emigrant ships were crowded but they offered chance for a new life: during the years of the famine on average 200-250,000 people quitted Ireland each year.

BELOW: The Brooklyn Bridge — built mainly by Irish labor.

practical difficulty of crossing the Atlantic during wartime. Rates picked up again after the war but not to 19th century highs. These variations had significant impact on events in Ireland as well as America.

Within Ireland emigration patterns shifted somewhat in the late 19th century across the four provinces. Leinster always provided the least in terms of the proportion of its population who left. In the famine years south Ulster, along with the neighboring areas of north Connacht and the north-west corner of Leinster, led the way (ie. Monaghan, Cavan, Fermanagh, Mayo, Sligo, Roscommon, Leitrim and Longford), but many other counties sent large numbers, especially Cork, Clare, Galway and Antrim. By the 1870s many emigrants were still coming from the largely Catholic "outer" Ulster counties, with only slightly fewer, proportionately, from Munster and Connacht, but by the 1890s Ulster emigration dropped off considerably with Connacht men and women the most likely to leave, closely followed by those from Munster. At this stage rates of emigration for Leinster and Ulster were both quite low, with about 5 percent of the population leaving over the decade, while those for Munster and Connacht were 16 and 17 percent respectively.

With these shifting patterns came different types of emigrants. The largely destitute of the first wave of 1846–55 gave way to the better organized and educated of the second and third waves of the 1860s and 1880s. Most of the post-1860 emigrants did not leave in conditions of absolute degradation. The widespread introduction of steamships (these services had begun in the 1840s but only became affordable to the average emigré in the

ABOVE: While many of Irish stock ended up laboring, there were some notably successful families, the best-known of which is undoubtedly the Kennedys.

RIGHT: St Patrick's Roman Catholic Cathedral was started in 1858, opened in 1879, but only finished in 1906. At the time churchgoers complained it was too far out of town. Designed by James Renwick, patterned after the cathedral of Cologne, the towers rise to over 320ft.

1860s), cut the journey from four weeks to ten days. Their steam power also allowed much better heating and cooking facilities, and the crossing was generally less hygienically horrific, while established family networks in the US often provided the money to pay for it.

By the 1880s most new emigrants had no personal recollection of the famine and many were instead familiar with the commercialized modern world of railroads and telegraphs. Nearly all Irish migrants also had advantages of language not enjoyed by other European immigrants. Up to a million Irish speakers did go to America before 1880, but most were bilingual and those who were not usually adopted English very quickly. Very few passed on their Irish language to second generations and the communities which continued to use Irish in America were isolated — notably the miners of the Schuykill valleys in Pennsylvania and the settlements on Beaver Island in Lake Michigan. The pressures of American economic individualism and alien urban surroundings made wholesale reproduction of Irish ways unlikely. Irishness was not wilfully abandoned but necessarily transformed in the pressure cooker of the most rapidly developing country in

the world. It is to these fledgling communities that we should now turn.

THE STRUCTURE OF IRISH-AMERICAN COMMUNITIES

The Irish immigrants generally became an urban people even though they had usually come from rural areas in Ireland. Settlement concentrated on the north-eastern seaboard from Maryland to southern Maine, and then westwards into the industrial and mining centers of the midwest. The wide-open spaces of the prairies did not, on the whole, appeal to a convivial people whose rural landscape had been on a much more intimate scale. New York, Massachusetts, Pennsylvania, Ohio, New Jersey and then Michigan, Illinois and Indiana were the heartlands of Irish America — followed later by California. Within this area it was the big cities — especially New York, Boston, Chicago, Philadelphia, Baltimore, St. Louis and San Francisco — which became the most Irish in character, but all the towns in this broad north-eastern area (and many far beyond) had their Irish communities. Irish laborers often traveled in search of work or stayed on in a far-off town after laboring on a newly-constructed railroad or canal.

Early communities were often initially based on a shared Irish locality, which could form a more important focus for identity than a generalized Irishness. Indeed, distaste for those from another part of Ireland was often pronounced, with people from Connacht particularly looked down upon by other Irish-Americans. However, the challenges facing the Irish in their new American homes, including anti-Irish prejudice, gradually gave them a common purpose. Within the cities, neighborhoods were constructed around groups of blocks which soon became parishes once a church had been built. The family was important, and as marriage came at a younger age than in Ireland, the number of children was high. The appalling conditions of squalor and dirt led to high infant mortality rates and low life expectancy (perhaps as low as 22 in 1850s' Boston). Diseases such as Typhus, Cholera, Typhoid, Dysentry and Tuberculosis were rampant. Some cities were healthier than others (Boston, with its disgusting cellars was notably worse than Philadelphia in this respect) but all had their wretched corners.

These conditions inevitably led to sickness and widowhood, which in the harsh world of pre-welfare state capitalism created the need for mutual aid societies. These fostered community spirit and co-operation, as did local volunteer fire companies, which were vital in the early wooden tenement slums (or "barracks") thrown up in New York. Membership of militia companies and Irish nationalist organizations enhanced Irish-American identity as well as maintaining links with the old country, and voluntary organizations, such as the Ancient Order of Hibernians, promoted lavish celebrations of St. Patrick's Day, dances and picnics. Out of all this activity, however, there are two organizations which stand out as iconic of Irish America. The Catholic Church and the Democratic Party "machines."

The Catholic Church was a vital unifying institution for many of the emerging Irish-American communities. It

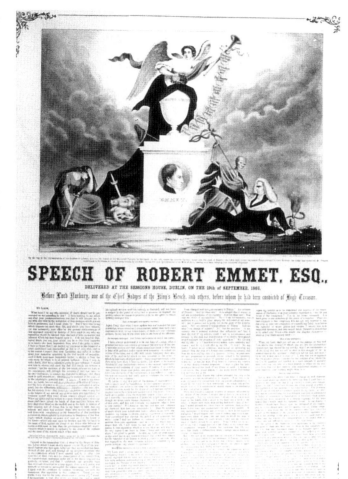

SPEECH OF ROBERT EMMET, ESQ.,
DELIVERED AT THE SESSIONS HOUSE, DUBLIN, ON THE 19th of SEPTEMBER, 1803.

gave Irish emigrants a link with their previous lifestyles, and the hardship, disease and economic uncertainty of the immigrants' new lives created an obvious need for its consoling role. The usual account of Irish-American Catholicism stresses devout, clannish, urban parishes under the somewhat authoritarian control of the local priest — often recently imported from the mother country. There is much truth in this image, but the degree of devotion displayed by Irish-Americans differed markedly. In predominantly Irish towns, where the church tended to be in Irish control, church attendance and emotional attachment was high. The presence of an overt anti-Catholic Protestant population (as in Boston) could also spur a strong, defensive Catholic affiliation — but, on the whole, the huge cosmopolitan cities such as New York often allowed religious laxity to develop in their more secular, anonymous spaces.

Of course, the Irish were not the only Catholics in America, and they often settled in established, mixed parishes under the pastoral care of American or recently arrived European priests. Hence, Catholicism could also be an unifying force. The devotion and commitment of such priests to their Irish parishioners (who were often deemed quite lax by European standards) impressed Irish immigrants and reminded them that their faith had a genuinely "Catholic" and not just a provincial Irish nature. In the brave new world of America, Catholics with German, French, Spanish, Latin American, Italian and Polish roots abounded. The Irish were the largest single ethnic group-

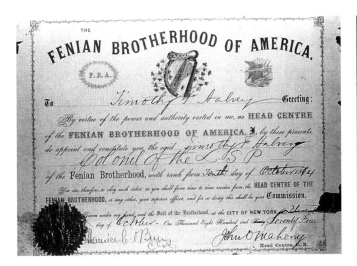

LEFT: *"Speech of Robert Emmet, Esq, delivered at the Sessions House, Dublin, on the 19th of September, 1803." Through his famous abortive rising of 1803, Emmet was especially remembered by Irish nationalists in both Ireland and American. This poster was published in Philadelphia in the late 19th century.*

ABOVE: *A commission appointing Timothy F. Halvey colonel of the Legion of St. Patrick, a military adjunct of the Fenian Brotherhood of America, signed by John O'Mahony, October 11, 1874. The Fenians were named by O'Mahony in honour of the ancient Fianna warriors of Celtic Ireland.*

RIGHT: *Richard Croker, nicknamed "Boss," grew up in New York and became head of Tammany Hall and the New York Democratic Party (the Democrats became the chief vehicle of Irish-American power in the cities). He made a fortune and returned to Ireland in 1907. He would return again to the USA and die there in 1922.*

ing of Catholics for many years after the famine, but the Vatican, and the American hierarchy, were not prepared to tailor their church to Irish needs alone. Indeed the Vatican was slow to recognize the demographic shifts in both the creation of new bishoprics and in the appointment of Irish-American bishops. Irish-Americans were under-represented at the highest levels of the church until the late 19th century, and Chicago, Philadelphia and Boston were only given archbishops in the 1870s.

At a lower level, however, Irish-American Catholics were soon building their own churches, and not just local parish ones. New York's Gothic Revival St. Patrick's Cathedral, designed in 1859 by James Renwick, was an impressive demonstration of growing Irish-American power and prosperity. They also created their own schools from an early date, often prompted by dislike of the conditions of public-funding — such as the use of the Protestant King James version of the Bible instead of the Catholic Douay edition. These schools, which existed outside the state structure, were funded by private donations and provided the education which enabled entry into the professions by the turn of the century. Orphanages and hospitals soon followed, as Irish Catholic communities became adept at providing for their own needs.

In order to gain a measure of control over their harsh environment, Irish-Americans also organized politically. Their power structures were a curious mixture of the modern and the tribal. Full use was made of modern American democracy, which in terms of votes made the poorest Irish-American as important as the richest Anglo-Saxon Protestant. The Irish political "machines" realized quickly that numbers counted, and in the strongholds of New York, Chicago, Boston, Philadelphia, Baltimore, St. Louis, Kansas City and San Francisco, there were enough Irishmen to seize control of city government for long periods. Within these machines, cutting-edge party organization merged with the politics of personal fiefdom and patronage. The resources of city government, such as building contracts and jobs in the police, were managed according to the criteria of loyal service to the party machine, blatant ethnic favoritism and bribery. There was more than a faint whiff of ancient Gaelic kingship in the networks of family and friends which supported the system, and unsurprisingly, high-minded Anglo-Saxons, both conservative and radical, found it rather distasteful.

In many respects it was, but as a defensive reaction to poverty and prejudice it was perfectly understandable. Corruption and inefficiency were rife, merit often irrelevant, and fawning obedience to the "Boss" the norm. But the system did have its attractions. Problems with debt, rent arrears or unemployment could be directed to a known figure, within a clearly understood hierarchy, who might help you out if able and inclined to do so in return for future obligations. It also provided jobs for the boys. Famous practitioners included "Boss" Richard Croker, William Tweed and Charles Murphy, all of New York's Tammany Hall (the "machine" system as a whole is often known by the name of this hall). Also worthy of note are

Richard Daley of Chicago and Frank Hague of Jersey City — who famously declared "I am the Law" in a manner worthy of Louis XIV.

THE IRISH-AMERICAN CONTRIBUTION

Irish-Americans played a vital role in building modern America. As well as filling the factories of the north-east, the railroads, roads, bridges, canals, sewers, dams, buildings and all the other elements of a modern industrialized nation were built largely by Irish labor. The spectacular economic growth of 19th century America which had encouraged Irish immigration, was then pushed along even faster by Irish labor. An explosion in railroad mileage from 3,000 in 1840 to 30,000 in 1860 coincided precisely with the heaviest years of famine and immediate post-famine immigration. Irish labor contributed heavily to the first transcontinental rail link and the Eire Canal. Such work, while brutally hard, provided a welcome escape route from the squalor and overcrowding of the seaboard cities. For those who remained, there was no shortage of construction work. The Brooklyn Bridge, one of the greatest feats of 19th century engineering, was built mainly by Irish labor, and by enabling America's most rapidly-growing city to expand onto Long Island, it fueled even faster economic and population growth in the city. From 100,000 people in 1810, New York had expanded to over a million by 1871. In this year another great, if tragic, opportunity arose for Irish labor. A fire in Chicago destroyed much of the city center and provided the opportunity for a new type of architecture. The skyscrapers that began to rise in Chicago, and then New York, from the 1880s would not have been possible without Irish muscle power. Of course, given the safety regulations of the day, many Irish-Americans lost their lives on these and other construction projects.

Yet despite this contribution to America, "native" Americans (or rather, established immigrants of British Protestant background) feared cultural contamination. The Know-Nothing party became the focus of this Nativism, which reached a peak during the famine exodus (Scots-Irish distancing from their fellow Irishmen also accelerated around this time). One of its leaders, Samuel Morse, likened the influx to mud being thrown into pure water. Weary Irish emigrants had merely fled from British indifference to American hostility. As in the British Isles, anti-Catholic prejudice contributed heavily to this anti-Irish sentiment. The Anglo-Saxon American elite, despite flowery constitutional statements to the contrary, had always seen America as an essentially Protestant country. The 17th century English fear of despotism and popery had survived remarkably intact in their transatlantic ancestors of the 19th century. However, they were in a less threatened position than the Anglo-Irish Protestant and could afford, eventually, to be more accommodating. Unthreatened by an overwhelming Catholic majority with a long memory of dispossession in a small island, the "native" Americans enjoyed an unassailable political and economic hegemony in a fluid, vast and expanding country. There was plenty of land and plenty of work for all. Nativism lingered in the background but gradually lost its edge.

Part of the reason it did so was the distraction of the Civil War and the task of reconstruction which followed. This vast conflict, which involved three million combatants (620,000 of whom died), provided a theater for Irish-Americans to show their courage. Irishmen fought and distinguished themselves on both sides, although their patterns of settlement dictated that the majority found their way into the Union armies. Being on the winning side helped assimilation. The Irish-American involvement was not just limited to cannon fodder. Both Ulysses Grant and "Stonewall" Jackson had Irish, albeit Protestant, ancestry. As well as strengthening the bond of Irish-Americans with their new state, the Civil War also provided trained and

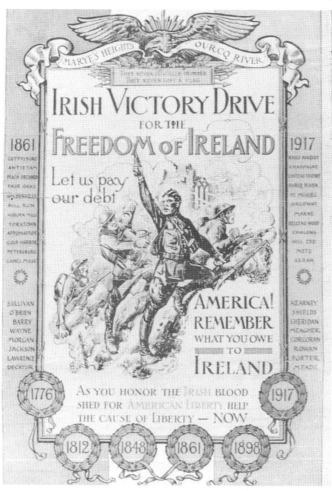

ABOVE: "Irish victory drive for the freedom of Ireland." This color poster, published in New York in 1917, is soliciting support for the republican cause. It lists battles in the USA and Europe in which Irishmen took part.

RIGHT: John O'Mahony led the Fenian Brotherhood in an abortive invasion of British territory in North America — Canada — in April 1866. An 800-strong army, composed mainly of veterans from the US Civil War, led by General John O'Neill was roundly defeated.

DAIL EIREANN'S MESSAGE TO DE VALERA

On the 29th June, 1920, the following message, proposed by Arthur Griffith, and unanimously agreed to by the Dail, was despatched to President De Valera in America:

"DAIL EIREANN, assembled in full session in Dublin to-day, unanimously re-affirms the allegiance of the Citizens of Ireland to your policy, expresses complete satisfaction with the work you have performed and relies with confidence upon the great American Nation to accord recognition to the REPUBLIC OF IRELAND now in fact and in law established."

ABOVE LEFT: "Dail Eireann's message to De Valera." The Dail's address to de Valera reaffirms its satisfaction with his policy in the US; June 29, 1920.

ABOVE: A manuscript letter circulated by de Valera in the US soliciting support for establishing the Irish Press, *February 1930.*

RIGHT: During 1919 John Devoy, a longstanding Irish-American leader, would clash with de Valera on the latter's trip to raise precious funds for the fledgling government of Ireland. This photograph is an 1871 view of a number of Irish nationalists: from left to right — John Devoy, Charles Underwood O'Connell, Harry S. Mulleda, Jeremiah O'Donovan Rossa, and Captain John McClure.

experienced soldiers, who would have an impact on Ireland in the Fenian rising of 1867.

During the 1870s and 1880s, Irish-Americans began their slow climb up the social scale. As new waves of immigrants from eastern and southern Europe arrived to take on the most menial physical jobs, many (although by no means all) Irish families achieved a higher position in the pecking order. "Wild" and "comic" Irish stereotypes remained strong, as did the reputation for drunkenness, but the vicious racialism of the 1850s abated. Irishwomen in domestic service and textile factories became nurses or sought gentility. From their jobs as miners, factory workers and laborers, Irishmen could aspire to the police force or civil service. A few even made fortunes in construction or climbed the greasy pole of national politics. These "lace curtain Irish" became the object of ridicule and satire from the old Anglo-Saxon Protestant elites, who still dominated the country in terms of power and wealth, but there were growing numbers of powerful and wealthy Irish-Americans by the end of the century.

Another way out of the mire was through sport and entertainment. The boxing legend John L. Sullivan, who became World Heavyweight Champion in 1883, did much to enhance that sport's standing and encouraged other young "fighting Irishmen" to follow in his footsteps. Baseball was full of Irish-Americans around the turn of the century, both as players and managers. Michael Kelly thrilled crowds on the field, while John Joseph McGraw led the New York Giants to success for many years. One who straddled both worlds was Charles Comiskey, player and later owner of the Chicago White Sox. Irish-American actors and songwriters, like George Cohan, also entertained the nation with such popular and patriotic ditties as "Over There," "Give My Regards to Broadway" and "I'm a Yankee Doodle Dandy."

By the early 20th century, the distinctive traits of Irish America were noticeably diverging from those of their homeland. Sentimentality and clannishness remained common to both in popular image, but it was joined by a hard-working, aggressive, ambitious, abrasive edge in Irish-Americans which, rightly or wrongly, was not generally ascribed to the Irish back home. Journalists, most notably Mark Sullivan and Finley Peter Dunne, reflected

increasing self-confidence and respectability. Dunne, in being able to mock his own community in his popular "Mr. Dooley" column, showed that it had come of age, while Sullivan made the transition from popular journalism to become the most respected political commentator of his day. Irish-American politicians were also making a serious assault on national power, notably Alfred E. Smith who became Governor of New York in 1918. After narrowly missing out on the Democratic presidential nomination of 1922 because of his strong anti-KKK stance, he did receive the nomination in 1928, but lost to Hoover during a time of great economic prosperity. Anti-Irish, anti-Catholic prejudice was still significant when it came to the top job, and this was not overcome until 1960, when the educated, urbane and rich John F. Kennedy was narrowly elected President.

THE AFFECT OF IRISH-AMERICANS ON IRELAND

The affect on Ireland of a numerous and increasingly wealthy Irish-American community was profound. Feelings of bitterness towards England festered in exile and combined with nostalgic memories of Ireland. Ever since the United Irish emigrants had established themselves as lawyers, publishers and political activists in America, there had been critical interaction with Irish politics from across the Atlantic. The repeal movement of O'Connell in the early 1840s received support from Irish-Americans (often organized by surviving United Irishmen such as MacNeven), and from the late 1850s onward fundraising in America was an essential and lucrative part of any nationalist enterprise, whether constitutional or revolutionary.

After the famine strong anti-Englishness naturally increased, and these sentiments were focused by John O'Mahony (see Chapter 1) in the Fenian movement. Safe distance from Ireland encouraged an exaggerated rhetoric and made it easier for American Fenians to take a harder line than those closer to British military might. This idealism, impatience and anger could inspire both action and violent infighting within the Fenian movement, but there is no doubting the bravery and sincerity of some Irish-American republicans. Eagerness to get at England even inspired pointless invasions of Canada in

ABOVE: "Toward America for Relief" — a 1920s' poster. The poverty of Ireland did not end with independence.

RIGHT: Immigrants learn to salute the flag: a generation of Irish men and women would flee the country, but few forgot their homeland. Pilgrimages back to Ireland would become increasingly popular.

1866 and 1870, and it was Irish-American Civil War veterans such as Colonel Kelly who provided much of the leadership and impetus for the failed 1867 Fenian rising in Ireland and Britain. After its founding in New York by Jerome Collins later that year, Clan na Gael became the new focus for Irish-American revolutionary Republicanism. Its guiding light after his release from prison in 1871 was John Devoy, who published *The Gaelic American* to rouse Irish-American support for revolutionary nationalism. From 1877 Clan na Gael recognized the Supreme Council of the IRB as the provisional "government" of Ireland and it continued in active existence down to independence. Its activities included the rescue of Fenians from transportation to Australia, dynamite campaigns in England in the 1880s, gun-running for the 1916 Easter Rising and, of course, fundraising.

The importance of Irish-American support was recognized by both Parnell and de Valera — who had American connections of their own (in Parnell's case his mother; in de Valera's, American birth). Each of them made trips to America to drum up support. Parnell's visit in 1880 inspired the National League of America to raise huge sums for the Land League, both for the relief of distress caused by food shortages and to back the Land War. Parnell was invited to address the House of Representatives on the issue, which enhanced his own reputation and increased awareness of Irish grievances in mainstream American politics. Furthermore, he tried to engage America in Irish affairs (a tactic of Irish nationalists which continues to this day). His justification was persuasive. "When the task is thrown upon America of feeding a people who have been driven into starvation by ruinous and unjust laws, surely you acquire a right to express your opinion very freely on the character of those laws and on the policy of maintaining them." In other words, American influence should be brought to bear on Britain to restore Irish rights.

The Home Rule Party was always dependent on American dollars, and Sinn Fein, which effectively replaced it in 1918, needed them even more to fund its fledgling republic. De Valera's trip to America in 1919 was successful in this respect, but it failed in its other

purpose — to secure American recognition of Irish nationhood and a seat at the Versailles peace conference. President Wilson even refused to meet de Valera, and Irish-Americans took this as a snub to their community. As a result they formed a vital part of the coalition which successfully opposed US involvement in the League of Nations, and thereby inadvertently destabilized the post-war European peace settlement. Such episodes demonstrate the growing power of Irish-Americans within the Democratic Party, and Sinn Fein was eager to use this power. Ironically, Sinn Fein was, however, violently opposed to the means of its rise — emigration.

There were serious negative aspects to emigration for Ireland, not least the constant drain of talent, energy and youth to the US. Given the intense pressure on the land in many areas — such as Connacht — emigration provided a safety valve for excess population and can be seen as a crucial element in the stability of the social and economic system. It also provided an inflow of American money from departed relatives which supported inefficient land holding and agriculture, but there was a deep and enduring sadness at the ever-present prospect of separation from loved ones. Second and third sons, as well as daughters whose parents could not afford a dowry, were effectively bred for emigration in parts of Ireland. Their youthful help was needed on the small family farm, but to keep that farm intact for the "stem" family, they must either leave or accept the status of unmarried wage laborer on the family holding — many chose the former.

It was this wastage that the Dail tried to stop during the War of Independence. Emigration was banned, and the IRA even raided hotels in Liverpool to confiscate the tickets, money and passports of those hoping to go. The effect of a temporary restriction on emigration on social and political stability could be significant. The years leading up to the Land War and independence were characterized by low emigration due to economic recession in America and World War I. This left a surplus of disgruntled young men, with little prospect of work or advancement and few doubts about who was to blame. However, emigration always recovered again after a few years, and it was still a common escape from rural poverty and boredom until quite recently. The American connection was as strong as ever when Ireland became a republic in 1949, and the enduring bond of affection and admiration for the United States among the Irish remains to this day. Similarly Irish-Americans retain their attachment and affection for their ancestral home. Pilgrimages to Ireland in search of their roots have never been more popular.

RIGHT: An image of one of the best-remembered moments of Irish-American involvement in the Fenian activity of 1867. Colonel Kelly, an Irish-American Civil War veteran, was "acting Chief Executive of the Irish Republic." His rescue from a prison van in Manchester led to the shooting of a police sergeant when a Fenian tried to shoot the lock off the van door. Three Fenians who had been present but who had not fired were tried and executed for murder. These "Manchester Martyrs" achieved more for the Fenians by their executions than they could have hoped to from their poorly-planned rising. The propaganda value was immense and the executions were long remembered as an infamous case of British injustice.

WORKING LIFE

ABOVE: Tram tracks are in evidence in this photograph of Donegall Place, which leads off Donegall Square in the heart of Belfast, towards Royal Avenue and St Anne's Cathedral.

PREVIOUS PAGE: A boy poses with a donkey carrying a heavy burden of turf in baskets. Note the rocky soils and mountainous terrain of this beautiful but somewhat bleak Connemara landscape in Co. Galway.

RIGHT: A young girl piles dried blocks of turf. The toe protruding from her flimsy shoe and worn-out sweater show the enduring poverty of Connemara life.

This chapter will try to delve a little behind the public face of Ireland. The politicians, poets and patriots have their place, but their activities and achievements often tell us little about what life was really like for ordinary people. For many, it was always about hard work in the field or the factory — or hardship brought on by the lack of it. However, the Irish century 1845–1945 saw the working life of town and country change dramatically. Better communications by road and rail, the shift from manual labor to mechanization and labor-extensive pastoral farming on the land, the decline of cottage industries and the growth (albeit limited) of industry in the cities all made their mark. However, there were also customs of social life, diet, leisure, sport and the like which were not much changed in the 1950s from the mid-19th century. And whatever the nature of the work, the Irish have always had a little time for relaxation and talk. They are a sociable people, and their love of good conversation, song and storytelling (however clichéd it sounds) continues to this day. Much Irish social life centered on the pub, but home and church had their place too, and in a country which remained predominantly rural throughout this period, such sociability could often be accommodated within the communal tasks and slower rhythm of country life. It is to these changes and continuities that the pictures and words of this chapter now turn.

AGRICULTURE AND RURAL LIFE

As we have seen in Chapter 1, there were considerable changes in the agricultural structure of Ireland between the famine and independence. These changes had three main strands: the transfer of ownership from landlord to tenant, the consolidation of farms which reversed a pre-famine trend of fragmentation, and the shift from tillage to pasture. These trends were made possible by the massive drop in population caused by the famine and continuing emigration. Both of these reduced pressure on the land and enabled the more prosperous tenant farmers to consolidate or increase the size of their farms, before eventually buying them out with the aid of a succession of land acts. As a result, with the exception of parts of the west, the number of laborers and small cottiers subsisting on a few acres decreased dramatically, while comfortable, small "strong farmers," with farms of 10 to 30 acres, became the norm.

Alongside these changes, naturally, came a different attitude to landlords. Farmers had shown growing solidarity and belligerence since the 1850s with the formation of groups like the Irish Tenant League. This was a coalition of small local tenant rights groups who sought lower rents (to be decided by independent valuation), greater security of tenure (to make eviction more difficult), and the nationwide adoption of the "Ulster custom" (which allowed tenant farmers to "sell" their interest in the land to the next tenant). The league was short-lived and ineffective, but a real trial of strength between farmers and the landlords came with the Land War of 1879–82. This pivotal event destroyed the old deferential relationship

ABOVE: An old weather-beaten woman feeding her chickens. Small numbers of poultry were often vital to survival in hard times and would be brought inside with the family in the poorer one or two-roomed dwellings.

RIGHT: The village carpenter building a table in Dunboyne, Co. Meath, around 1950. Even at the end of our period cottage industries such as this formed a vital part of the village community.

between landlord and tenant and began the transformation of the Irish agricultural system from landlordism to widespread ownership.

The Land War was really a mixture of two somewhat different struggles. Initially it was largely a struggle for survival in the west between landlords and starving peasant farmers and laborers. This gradually became fused with an attempt by larger tenant farmers in more prosperous areas to secure better terms. The outcome was Gladstone's Land Act of 1881, which set the slow train to tenant ownership in motion. The act itself was relatively ineffective in the short term. The 25 percent down payment required resulted in fewer than 1,000 farmers taking the opportunity to buy their land. However, the independent assessment of rents and security of tenure established by the act effectively acknowledged the right of farmers to a stake in the land they worked. The Ashbourne Act of 1885 speeded up the transfer of ownership, but it would not be completed until the early 20th century — in particular the years following the Wyndham Land Act of 1903 and its extension in 1909. This highly effective legislation allowed tenants to buy

ABOVE: Two small boys carrying water back to their home. The boy on the left looks like he has put on his Sunday best for the photograph — even if he has grown a few inches since he first wore the clothes!

BELOW: Another hard-worked donkey — this time pulling an old woman and her milk in Co. Mayo.

their land using government loans for 100 percent of the value of their property, which was then repaid at rates up to 20 percent lower than the rent. The take-up rate was dramatic. In 1876 four-fifths of Ulster, for example, was owned by about 800 landlords, by the 1920s nearly all farmers owned their own land.

The move to tenant ownership was partly driven by the idea that once farmers owned their own land they would become more efficient. This did not really happen. The size of farms remained too small for significant economies of scale — but Irish agricultural backwardness should not be over-stressed. The natural comparison to Britain is misleading, as its commercialized and advanced agriculture was not the norm in most of Europe. As early as 1850, three-quarters of Irish farming was commercial rather than subsistence. Indeed, by general European standards Irish agriculture, although very variable, was reasonably efficient by the late 19th century.

The new land system also encouraged a shift from tillage to pasture in most of the country, although this was driven as much by price changes as anything else. At the beginning of our period potatoes, livestock and grain each accounted for roughly a third of Irish agricultural production. By 1914 livestock alone made up three-quarters. In many areas damp conditions or poor soils had always been better suited to cattle and sheep than wheat or barley, and as the relative price levels changed in favor of livestock, marginal areas became less attractive for tillage. Overall, income per acre was still considerably lower from livestock farming, but so were costs (especially labor costs). As a result, similar levels of profit could be made — with far less effort. As cattle farming became

TOP: Building haystacks in Co. Wicklow. In the drier, sunnier, southeast a more comfortable rural life based on mixed or commercial arable farming was possible.

ABOVE: A farmer in the north of Co. Dublin brings home the hay, as well as some local children, while smoking a cigarette a few inches above his highly combustible load!

RIGHT: Harvest time in Co. Roscommon. Shirt sleeves are the order of the day for this back-breaking work as a farmer reaps his crop using an old-fashioned hand-held sickle.

more profitable, a class of large "ranchers" emerged on lands previously used for small potato patches. These graziers were much criticized for forcing peasants off the land and would have their cattle "houghed" (ie. their hamstrings severed) during the Land War.

Aside from these long-term trends, it is difficult to give a general picture of Irish rural life, however, for it could be very different in different places. In the far west, for example, life was often harsh, damp and windblown. The thin, rocky soils, low levels of sunshine and high rainfall were always unsuitable for grain production. The diet in these areas consisted mainly of potatoes. This was supplemented by a little milk, bacon, mutton or fish (and in some coastal areas by oysters, which used to be a poor man's food). For fish the wild Atlantic had to be braved, often in the somewhat flimsy constructions of skin and wood known as coracles or curaghs. This was a precarious business and Synge's account of a journey in a curagh shows just how close to disaster the Aran Islanders who used such vessels came each day.

"As we worked out into the sound we began to meet another class of waves, that could be seen for some distance towering above the rest. When one of these came in sight, the first effort was to get beyond its reach. The steersman began crying out in Gaelic 'Siubhal, siubhal' ('run, run'), and sometimes, when the mass was gliding towards us with horrible speed, his voice rose to a shriek. Then the rowers themselves took up the cry, and the curagh seemed to leap and quiver with the frantic terror of a beast till the wave passed behind it or fell with a crash beside the stern . . . I could see the steersman quivering with the excitement of his task, for any error in his judgement would have swamped us."

Indeed many islanders were lost at sea and the grief of their families was expressed in terrible keening (wailing) at their funerals. (Synge's play, *Riders to the Sea*, gives some insight into this grieving.) In these western, Gaelic-speaking lands, fairies and magic were part of the fabric of life well into this century, giving it a romantic appeal to an anglicized, urban, Irish middle class in search of a pure Irish identity. For the islanders themselves, the harsh life was only made bearable by a superstitious, almost pagan, form of religion, by the violent beauty of the landscape, by conversation and storytelling at a warm fireside, and the comfort of whiskey or poteen. As younger generations came into contact with the popular culture and material well-being of the outside world, they increasingly left for the nearest town or emigrated to America to escape their hard, primitive existence.

Aran Island poverty was extreme, but in many parts of

RIGHT: The slim canvas and wood curaghs of these Blasket islanders are very similar to those used by Synge on the Aran Islands. Their long oars are leaning against the rocks in the background and lobster pots are piled up on the slipway, which had probably been built by the Congested Districts Board to encourage the local fishing industry.

TOP LEFT: *Loading hay onto a horse-drawn cart.*

ABOVE: *Thatching in the small town of Oughterard in Co. Galway.*

LEFT: *Rabbits supplement the diet of tinkers in Co. Donegal.*

ABOVE RIGHT: *Two men twining rough, home-made rope in Co. Donegal.*

BELOW RIGHT: *Threshing with the aid of an early mechanical device in Cavan. The grain is coming out of the bottom left to be put into sacks while the stalks are being forced out of the right-hand end.*

ABOVE: The woman-to-fish ratio seems rather high as five country women attempt to sell their catch at an improvized fish market.

BELOW: A thatched roof serves a dual purpose on an Aran Island cottage. The white marks are mackerel drying in the sun.

RIGHT: Bartley Flaherty baits his spillet before going fishing on the Aran island of Innishmaan. Note the rough sheepskin boots, or "pampooties," on his feet.

the country a 19th century cabin was a dismal affair. A single or double-roomed building was commonly shared by a family or six or even eight. The better ones were made of stone and thatched with straw, and may even have had a glazed window; the worst were made entirely of turf with a single open doorway. The floor was simply earth, and the occupants slept on mats of straw — often together under the same cover. Pigs, dogs, geese, chickens and ducks shared this shelter. A pile of peat turf for fuel would sit in the corner by the fire, and there would be very little furniture — perhaps a rough wooden table and a few chairs. Over the fire a cauldron of potatoes might be boiling for dinner, and if some milk, herring or bacon accompanied them the poorer inhabitants would count themselves lucky. Tea became popular for those who could afford it, but bread was always rare in many parts of the country. As well as potatoes, these peasants would grow oats and cabbages where they could and keep a cow or two for milk if possible.

One animal that was at home even among windswept rocks was the sheep. Hence wool was rarely scarce and in many areas most clothes were usually made from wool which was scoured, carded and spun in the home. When dyed, these could bring some color to the muted greys, greens and browns of the rural landscape. Synge frequently pointed out the bright red of the shawls and petticoats of the Aran Islanders. In some parts of the country, and especially Ulster, linen was used. It would be left out in fields to 'bleach' in the sun and then would be spun in homes. This putting-out system was a vital source of income in the province, but it gradually died out as steam-powered mills made it more economic to produce linen in Belfast factories.

In the south-east counties of Wexford, Waterford, Carlow and Kilkenny, a warmer, drier climate, along with more fertile soils, allows crops like wheat and barley to flourish. A far more comfortable rural life has always characterized these counties, and it is no coincidence that the Anglo-Normans chose their lush river valleys — the Nore, Suir, Barrow and Slaney — to settle first. For the bulk of the country, however, dairy and cattle farming was (and still is) the norm. The lush, wet grasslands of the south and center of the island are ideal for this sort of agriculture. Many medium and small farmers went in for mixed cattle and arable farming and settled into a comfortable, though hardly prosperous, existence which made innovation and increases in efficiency unlikely. Maintaining the farm intact for the eldest son, who was often quite old when he took it over, became the *raison d'être* of rural life. Marriage came late and was often a somewhat mercenary affair, with detailed negotiations over the dowry, the number of cattle, and the value of land at the forefront of the transaction.

By the early 20th century, rural Ireland was well integrated with the modern, commercial, world economy. By 1914 3,500 miles of railways had been built, making the Irish network one of the most dense in the world. The English language was spoken by almost the entire population, giving the people easy access to the commercial culture of the USA as well as Britain. As literacy was high

TOP: The journey to a creamery in Co. Limerick.

ABOVE: A creamery at Charleville, Co. Cork. Many Irish creameries were built by co-operatives under the guidance of Sir Horace Plunkett's Irish Agricultural Organisation Society founded in 1894. By 1904 there were 876 societies with an annual turnover of around £3 million.

ABOVE RIGHT: Patriarchal Ireland? Three Connemara women carry huge baskets of turf home while a middle-aged man stands idly by.

RIGHT: The characterful, weather-beaten faces of four fishermen in Courtown, Co. Wexford.

TOP: *A man drives his donkey down a country lane in Connemara. The bicycle was a common and relatively cheap way of getting around in rural Ireland.*

ABOVE CENTER: *The captain of this small steam boat in Connemara looks suspiciously at the photographer while his young assistant seems more interested in a sod of turf.*

ABOVE: *Mechanical threshing of grain in Killarney, Co. Kerry.*

RIGHT: *The small town of Clifden in Co. Galway is the unofficial capital of Connemara. These men are repairing one of its roads.*

— almost 90 percent — books, periodicals and newspapers flooded in, especially from Britain. The effects of this modernization on Irish rural life were profound. The wealth and security of those who could get hold of their own farms steadily increased, and mass-produced manufactured goods found their way into their homes in increasing numbers. The increasing dependence on a market economy also had its drawbacks and for others the effect could be devastating.

Firstly, as English was the language of the new system, the Gaelic language went into severe decline, although, ironically, literature in English also opened up parochial societies to political influences and perhaps made them more revolutionary and Nationalist than they might otherwise have been. Secondly, modernization made the rural economy more reliant on money and less self-sufficient. Such a system could entail great hardship with violent price changes beyond the control of the individual. For those without their own farms, which included younger children of farm-owning families, prospects were often bleak. Those with a little money or academic ability could emigrate with some confidence or seek a clerical job, but work on the land became ever scarcer with the shift to pasture. The market economy also disrupted old links of service and obligation between elite and poor which could, on occasion, provide some protection in times of scarcity. For the poor, the older forms of traditional economy, based on a mixture of subsistence farming on small plots, laboring and bartering had a diversity which allowed them to scrape out a living on the land. Increasingly they were forced to emigrate or move to the towns and cities. It is to life in these towns and cities we now turn.

INDUSTRY AND URBAN LIFE

The distinction between town and country in Ireland has always been less stark than in many other countries. With the exception of two medium-sized cities — Dublin and Belfast — the economy of the town was intimately linked to that of the country. Of the cities, only Belfast contained extensive factories and heavy industry. Brewers, tanners, wholesale merchants, provision dealers, butchers, shopkeepers, publicans and artisans of various descriptions were the lifeblood of Irish towns, and nearly all of these depended, in one way or another, upon agricultural produce. Most of urban Ireland was always, in a sense, rural. Irish industry was generally underdeveloped throughout this period and few towns contained a sizeable working-class urban proletariat which could divorce itself from country concerns.

There were notable exceptions. Industrialized areas grew up in Belfast, along the adjoining Lagan valley, and in Londonderry. These were based initially on the linen industry, which had traditionally been strong in the north of Ireland since the 18th century. Hampered by trade restrictions on wool by the British parliament until 1779, linen had been allowed to develop as an alternative. After the 1830s, mechanized power looms allowed an impressive expansion in the industry, especially in Belfast. Internal migration in search of work, partly as a

ABOVE: An old Connemara woman proudly shows off her beautiful quilt. Such skills often passed across the Atlantic with emigrants to become American as well as Irish traditions.

ABOVE LEFT: The "family" nature of cottage industries such as spinning wool is clearly brought out in this picture, as two sons help their mother at the wheel.

BELOW LEFT: An old woman spinning wool in Co. Donegal. Apart from enabling families to make their own clothes, these cottage industries provided a vital part of their income, especially in the 19th century.

consequence of the famine, fueled the city's growth and by 1850 Belfast had become the biggest trading port in Ireland, despite being considerably smaller than Dublin in terms of population (around 100,000 as opposed to 250,000). As the century progressed, Belfast expanded more rapidly than any other city in the British Isles, reaching a population total of around 340,000 by 1900. Its continued growth was now based on engineering and shipbuilding as much as linen. The engineering industry initially developed in response to the need for textile machinery in the mills, but it continued to prosper after the linen industry began to decline in the face of cheaper cotton clothing. Two of the leading manufacturers were George Horner, who set up the Clonard Foundry in 1859, and Steven Cotton, whose Brookfield Foundry was established six years later. Both men had come over to Belfast from Leeds in northern England.

Similarly the growth of shipbuilding was largely due

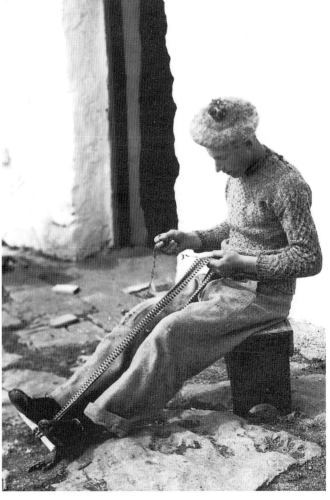

ABOVE: The "pampootie" was the traditional footwear of the Aran Islanders. Made of wet sheepskin, the finished article can be seen on the maker's own feet.

ABOVE RIGHT: Traditional crafts such as basket-weaving were handed down from generation to generation in the west of Ireland.

RIGHT: This young Aran islander is weaving a traditional belt called a croisanna.

FAR RIGHT: These women are dressed in their beautiful, decorative shawls for a special occasion — the confirmation of a group of local children.

TOP RIGHT: These homely cottages in Ardare, Co. Limerick, show that Irish rural life was not all turf cabins and misery. These would not look out of place in the most prosperous English village.

ABOVE: A day out in the country for a fashionably dressed group in the 1860s, although the tall beaver hats and silk dresses are hardly ideal for boat trip or a stroll in the woods.

LEFT: An increasing interest in tourism and the picturesque combined in this picnic outing to the Dargle valley on Lord Powerscourt's estate in Co. Wicklow, which became a popular summer destination for Dubliners.

ABOVE RIGHT: The awe-inspiring basalt columns of the Giant's Causeway in Co. Antrim were a very popular tourist destination for the growing populace of Belfast.

BELOW RIGHT: One of the most popular destinations for the increasing numbers of day trippers was the racecourse. This picture of Punchestown races, probably taken during the visit of Edward Prince of Wales in 1868, shows that all social ranks attended these meetings, from the obviously poor women at bottom right, to the ladies and gentlemen standing in their carriage above them to get a better view, and the large number of soldiers in uniform.

to the entrepreneurial and engineering skills of immigrants. Belfast's first shipyard had been founded in 1791 by the Presbyterian Scotsman William Ritchie, who built Belfast's first steamship in 1820 (with the suitably Scottish name of *Rob Roy*). Ritchie was an innovative shipbuilder, but the fledgling industry only became an important part of the Belfast economy after the emergence of Harland and Wolff in the 1860s. Edward Harland was an Englishman from Scarborough, Yorkshire. After learning his trade in Newcastle and Glasgow, he came over to work for Robert Hickson's ailing shipyard in 1854. He nearly left to set up his own yard near Liverpool in 1858, but Hickson gave him the chance to buy the company for £5,000 — part of which he raised from G. C. Schwabe, the uncle of Gustav Wilhelm Wolff. A German Jew educated in Liverpool, Wolff had been Hickson's assistant, and by 1860 Harland had entered into a formal partnership with him.

Harland and Wolff soon became one of the largest and most advanced shipbuilding firms in the world, inventing the "Belfast bottom" and pioneering the manufacture of larger and larger ships. They owed much of their success to William James Pirrie, a Canadian of Ulster stock who rose from apprentice to chairman between 1862 and the death of Harland in 1895. According to Wolff there was a somewhat unequal division of labor among the firm's three leaders. "Sir Edward builds the ships, Mr. Pirrie makes the speeches, and, as for me, I smoke the cigars." Pirrie did more than make speeches, and by the time of his own death in 1924 he was Belfast's leading businessman. The success of Harland and Wolff also inspired two of its employees, George Clark and Frank Workman, to set up another shipbuilding firm in 1880 — although Clark was also a Scot rather than a native of Belfast.

Symbolizing this industrial ethos, in 1885 a Trade Arch was erected in the center of Belfast with the inscriptions "Trade is the Golden Girdle of the World," and "Man goeth forth unto his work and to his labour unto the evening." Whether laboring unto the evening in the inferno of a steel foundry or the deafening noise of a mechanized mill was necessarily such a good thing never seems to have crossed the minds of these business leaders. The Victorian Protestant work ethic ruled supreme — and it was often very Protestant. The negative side of Belfast's business success was the growing sectarianism in the workplace. Belfast's Protestants had once been noted for their particularly tolerant attitude to Catholics, but from the 1850s anti-Catholic sectarian rioting became a recurring phenomenon. Encouraged by their bosses (although they needed little incentive) Belfast's Protestant ship workers made it well nigh impossible for Catholics to obtain skilled jobs at the yards, and discrimination was the norm in most industries. Catholics were a large and growing minority in Belfast from the famine onwards, but their status was distinctly second class. Local government was dominated by Protestants, and political power often went hand-in-hand with economic power. Harland became Lord Mayor and then Conservative MP for North Belfast. Wolff conveniently swapped the Star of David for the Orange sash, joining

TOP: The huge troughs in this picture contain fish which are being cured and packed into barrels in Ardglass, Co. Down.

ABOVE: The women working in this small weaving room are actually in the employ of a convent in Queenstown, Co. Cork. The distant look on the face of the woman on the right reminds us what tedious work this was.

ABOVE RIGHT: Members of the local fishing fleet and their families pose on the quayside at Ardglass, Co. Down.

BELOW RIGHT: The port of Waterford was a major outlet for the agricultural produce of the fertile south-eastern counties. This view of the town was taken in the 1860s and shows sailing ships still predominant. Steam would soon take over, however.

the Church of Ireland and becoming MP for East Belfast. Clark, in particular, was virulently anti-Catholic, and was heavily involved with the gun-running at Larne and the Ulster Volunteer Force.

While Ulster was the most industrialized of the four provinces, it remained largely rural throughout the period. The number of town dwellers jumped significantly from 10 to 40 percent of the population between 1841 and 1911, but that still left 60 percent of Ulster's population on the land. Furthermore, as in the rest of Ireland, many in this urban category actually lived in small market towns intimately connected with country life. Even Belfast was never huge by British and American standards, and its compactness meant that rural life was never too far away. Huddled beneath hills on either side, the working people of Belfast could easily climb up and enjoy the beauty of the countryside. And from the top of these hills, especially Cave Hill, the views across the city revealed the impact of the 19th century transformation, as Michael McLaverty describes in *Call My Brother Back*:

"At the top of the mountain they lay in the heather and gazed at Belfast spread out in the flat hollow beneath them, its lean mill chimneys stretched above the haze of smoke. Rows of red-bricked houses radiated on all sides and above them rose blocks of factories with many of their windows catching the sunlight."

If there could be a touch of wistful romance in a Victorian city viewed from afar, up close the real thing was quite different. This was especially true of Dublin. As well as its elegant Georgian squares, Dublin had some of the worst slums in Europe. Sean O'Casey, who came from them, was in less than romantic mood in this description of a Dublin street from *Inishfallen, Fare Thee Well*:

"Its roughly cobbled roadway beset with empty matchboxes, tattered straws, tattered papers, scattered mounds of horse-dung, and sprinkled deep with slumbering dust waiting for an idle wind to come an raise it to irritating life again."

Off the street, the houses led to an even grimmer story, "to tarnishing labour, to consumption's cough, to the writhings of fever, to bitter mutterings against life, and frantic calls on St. Anthony . . ."

Unlike Belfast, Dublin had little heavy industry to employ its poor. As in the smaller towns its chief business was the processing, distribution and export of agricultural produce, but on a larger scale. Brewing, distilling, glass and biscuit-making were among the major industries, and the biggest success story in Dublin was undoubtedly Arthur Guinness's brewery. In the 18th century Ireland imported most of its beer from Britain. By the 20th century Ireland was a net exporter of beer — most of it stout, a wonderful variation on the old British porter, made with burnt hops. Guinness arguably brought this technique of beer-making to perfection, producing one of the finest beers in the world. Dublin was, of course, also a major port, but it failed to industrialize in the way Belfast did.

ABOVE LEFT: The long structure surrounded by scaffolding on the left is a ship under construction in one of Belfast's famous shipyards. Belfast's two main yards, Harland and Wolff and Workman & Clark, were a vital part of the city's economy by the 1880s.

BELOW LEFT: The Titanic *was constructed by Harland and Wolff for the White Star line. This "unsinkable" ship was launched on May 31, 1911, and infamously went down on her maiden voyage to the USA.*

TOP: The seaside town of Bray on the edge of Dublin Bay in Co. Wicklow was transformed into a thriving tourist town by the rail link to Dublin opened in 1854.

ABOVE: A view over Cork in the late 19th century.

BELOW: The grand colonnaded frontage of the Ulster Railway terminal in Belfast opens out onto a muddy unpaved street and a more primitive form of transport.

LEFT: Fishermen attempt to erect a new mast on their vessel.

TOP RIGHT: The Dublin docks — these were one of the focal points of Ireland's most serious industrial dispute in 1913.

BOTTOM RIGHT: This Connemara weaver looks as if he has been weaving wool for centuries.

Many explanations have been put forward for this, such as a lack of natural resources (Ireland has no coal or iron), and a lack of Irish capital — but neither of these hampered Belfast. Equally spurious are the distinctions sometimes made between a Protestant work ethic in Belfast, and Catholic other-worldly lethargy in the south. Apart from the fact that many of Belfast's most successful business leaders were not from Ulster (although they were generally Protestants), many contemporaries actually criticized Dublin for being too materialistic. In comparison with Britain, there was a lack of industrial risk-taking in the south generally, but once again comparisons with Britain can be misleading. Britain was the exception during this period rather than the rule — remaining one of the three or four most advanced and industrialized countries in the world up to the end of our period. Also, within the logic of a greater British Isles economy, Ireland could be seen as playing a complementary agricultural role just like rural "regions" in other countries.

Dublin did have a fairly large middle class of professionals, and to a large extent the stature and financial rewards accorded to lawyers and doctors accounts for this entrepreneurial lethargy. A good doctor or lawyer could earn well over £1,000 a year, which was more than many small or medium firms could, and there was also the gentlemanly status which went along with it. Ironically, the desire to emulate British models of social hierarchy may carry more blame than any native "failings" in redirecting Irish talent and energy away from the business activity Ireland so desperately needed. Historians have been dubiously blaming the decline of British manufacturing (before it had actually started!) on the British elite's distaste for industry, but such attitudes arguably did more harm to Ireland than Britain by influencing its elite before it had any industry about which to be distasteful. The Gaelic League's distrust of most things English (which often included industrialization) also contributed to the anti-commercial attitude of the Dublin elite, which was shared by both Catholic and Anglican.

Dublin also had a high proportion of employees in the service and distribution industries, such as shopkeepers, publicans, teachers, clerks and civil servants. Before the Easter Rising this lower middle class was derided by Yeats and Joyce for its materialistic and petty outlook. According to Yeats, what could they do,

"But fumble in a greasy till
And add the halfpence to the pence
And prayer to shivering prayer, until
You have dried the marrow from the bone?"

Yet it was largely from these ranks that the revolutionaries of the 1916 rising were drawn. Yeats admitted as much in his panegyric to that event, expressing surprise in the bravery of these ordinary men that he had met,

". . . at the close of day
Coming with vivid faces
From counter or desk among grey
Eighteenth–century houses."

In the north, industry went into serious decline after partition although this was due to local difficulties and worldwide economic conditions rather than anything resulting from its new political status. During the 1920s, unemployment hovered around 20 percent, and after the Wall Street crash, world recession lead to unemployment of around 27 percent for most of the 1930s. Increased wartime production helped matters in the 1940s but unemployment remained much higher than in Britain. Industrialization in the Free State failed to materialize. The benefits of independence, which many thought would spur renewed growth, were economically negligible. Indeed, given the destruction and disruption of the Civil War — not to mention the futile and highly damaging trade war with Britain in the 1930s, which curtailed Ireland's chief export market for agricultural products — one could argue that independence was initially detrimental to Ireland's economy. The 1930s were a particularly bleak time, and high levels of urban poverty and unemployment continued to scar Dublin and other Irish cities until very recently.

Release from the stress and scarcity of urban life was often provided by drink and sport. The number of pubs in Ireland increased steadily over the period, but although there were twice as many per capita as in England by 1911 and an increase in annual beer consumption from 40 to 160 pints per person between 1841 and 1911, consumption was still slightly less per head than in England. Spirit drinking fell significantly but overall annual spending on alcohol rose to £15 million by World War I.

Another staple of Irish life was horse racing. This became a national obsession, reflecting the love of horses which the Irish of all classes have always had. Much horse racing took place on beaches, or makeshift steeplechase courses over fields, hedges, walls and ditches, but modern transportation allowed more and more Dubliners to escape from the city for a day out at the purpose-built racecourses springing up around Dublin.

At one end of the social scale was the Curragh. The 5,000 acres of open, unfenced grasslands and pasture in County Kildare was (and still is) the center of Irish flat racing. All of the Irish classics are held there, such as the Derby, the Oaks, the 1,000 and the 2,000 guineas. For centuries many of the world's finest racehorses have been bred and trained on the Curragh and racing there may date back 2,000 years. It is still circled by the large houses and stables which reflect the social exclusivity of the Curragh under British rule — when its race meetings were generally the preserve of officers from the nearby army camp and the Anglo-Irish social elite. Less exalted

Two photographs of Belfast in the early years of this century:

ABOVE LEFT: The boat for the resort of Bangor, east of Belfast on the Ards Peninsula, loads up at Donegall Quays.

LEFT: Horse trams and carriages on Victoria Street looking towards the Albert Memorial Clock Tower in the distance. Designed by W. J. Barre the tower was one of many built after the death of Queen Victoria's consort in 1861. Today the tower leans as a result of slight subsidence.

fare could be found at the racecourses of Leopardstown (probably the next most important racing center in Ireland), Fairyhouse (home of the Irish National) and Punchestown. All these, as well as a number of smaller courses, such as Navan, Naas and Bellewstown, are within easy day-trip range of Dublin — showing the astonishing demand for race meetings. Indeed there was at least one course (and often more) in nearly every county, Galway, Mallow, Thurles and Listowel being just a few of the better known ones. Often the high point of the local racing calendar would be a festival of racing, attracting amateur and professional alike. With music from a local band, free-flowing whiskey and porter, and the noise and color of a huge crowd, Irish race meetings in the 19th and early 20th century were often the local social high point.

Around the turn of the century, as in many other western countries, professional and amateur team sports began to attract large crowds in the larger towns. Rugby was popular, especially among the middle classes and the college-educated, but since the founding of the Gaelic Athletic Association in 1884, sports of British origin, such as football, were frowned upon. Hurling and Gaelic football soon took over as the national sports, and the big days for both games took place at Croke Park in north Dublin. Over 60,000 would crowd in to watch the All Ireland Finals in September between the county teams, or the Railway Cup Finals on St. Patrick's Day (March 17) fought out between teams representing Munster, Leinster, Connacht and Ulster. Such leisure activities testify to a slowly growing prosperity (although growth *was* slow until the 1960s) and a modern commercial lifestyle often very similar to that of America or the rest of western Europe and worlds away from pre-famine Ireland.

Between the famine and the 1950s life in Ireland had indeed changed dramatically in most respects. Schemes for state-provided health care, unemployment benefit and pensions were by no means generous, but they took the edge off poverty in both town and country. Buses and cars were slowly beginning to allow greater movement around the country and hence an escape from the sometimes claustrophobic atmosphere of village life. Child mortality was falling and consumption, which killed around 5,000 young adults a year, was finally being tackled. Radio, and soon television, would greatly assist this modernizing trend: a trend which would come to fruition under Sean Lemass in the 1960s. But change was slow and continuities remained. De Valera for one: he did not resign from his last stint as Taoisach until 1959. Emigration was still a running sore, bleeding the country of up to 50,000 — and mainly young people — in some years. The powerful Catholic Church still had great influence over social life and personal relationships, not to mention politics — the church's opposition to a state health care scheme for mothers and children had effectively caused the downfall of the coalition Fine Gael government in 1951. For many, especially in the country, the quiet rhythm of the seasons, the influence of the local priest, and the hard reality of friends and relations leaving for America still ordered their lives in a manner little changed from the previous century.

ABOVE LEFT: O'Connell Bridge, Dublin. This photograph is datable to within a few months of August 15, 1882 — when the O'Connell monument at left was unveiled — and 1883 when winged victories were added. The bridge replaced the hump-backed Carlisle Bridge and opened to traffic in 1880; it was from around this time that Sackville Street became known as O'Connell Street. Trams had been in operation since the 1870s (a horse-drawn vehicle is visible at right); electricity lit some streets and the city of Dublin — with a growing population of over a quarter of a million — was a busy and gracious city.

LEFT: The Custom House, Dublin; this Georgian building was erected between 1781 and 1791. The scene of fighting in the Rising, in 1921 Sinn Fein supporters celebrated their election victory by setting fire to it.

ABOVE: Dublin's covered market, between Drury Street and South Great George's Street, like Leadenhall in London, has been a hive of activity since it was erected.

RIGHT: A row of early Victorian cottages in Dun Laoghaire, formerly known as Kingstown in days when the British Army used the port as its main point of entry to Ireland.

ABOVE: Patrick Street, Cork, shows the pace of progress. LEFT the scene before trams, RIGHT electric trams share the street with horse-drawn transport.

RIGHT: Ireland's neutrality during World War II meant her cities did not suffer the aerial bombardment that flattened so much of mainland Britain's heritage. Despite this new building did go ahead during the period — here the Aras Mhic Dhiarmada CIE bus station which opened in 1948. ZD6880, nearest the camera, and three other buses pose under the Aras bus garage canopy.

BELOW: Collinstown airfield — previously used by both Royal Flying Corps and Royal Air Force — was chosen by the Irish government as Dublin's civil airport. On January 19, 1940, the official ceremony opened what was considered to be the grandest terminal in Europe, the architect — 25-year old Desmond Fitzgerald — receiving a gold medal for it from the Royal Institute of the Architects of Ireland. Aer Lingus, founded in 1936, started operations with a small fleet of de Havilland aircraft, receiving its first Douglas DC-3 on May 7, 1940; it had been prepared by Fokker in Amsterdam and flew out of the Netherlands under the noses of the invading German Army. After the war Aer Lingus blossomed and by 1950 the network expanded to Amsterdam and Paris as well as many locations on the mainland.

ARTS & LITERATURE

PREVIOUS PAGE: The flowering of Irish writing in our period saw many writers of international renown — George Bernard Shaw may not be as "Irish" as Joyce but he kept a keen eye on his homeland. This statue of him by Troubetzkoy is in the environs of the National Gallery of Ireland, to whom he bequeathed a third of his estate.

ABOVE: Marsh's Library is the oldest public library in Ireland, having been built in 1701 to the designs of Sir William Robinson, architect of much of Dublin Castle. This photograph shows a reader in the "cages," where scholars are locked in with the books.

RIGHT: Oliver Goldsmith — the great 18th cenury dramatist. This is a detail of the statue of him outside Trinity College's entrance.

Any review of the arts in Ireland between the famine and the Republic must inevitably focus on literature, and within that genre must inevitably be drawn to that remarkable renaissance in Irish writing which occurred between 1891 and 1921. Within this period Ireland produced five writers of international stature — Yeats, Wilde, Shaw, Joyce and Synge — and by the end of it another, Beckett, was emerging. Apart from these famous figures, the thriving Irish literary world produced many other talented dramatists, poets and novelists, such as Sean O'Casey, George Moore, Douglas Hyde and Lady Gregory, to name but a few. But there was more to Irish artistic life than literature, with interesting developments and talented artists in the fields of music and the visual arts during this period.

LITERATURE

Rather than the literature of Ireland, it perhaps makes more sense to speak of the literatures of Ireland. Culturally as well as politically there was, as F. S. L. Lyons has called it, a "battle of two civilisations." However, one thing these literatures often had in common, even more so than in other nations, was an intimate connection with the history and politics of the country. Since time immemorial an ancient bardic culture had celebrated the heroic deeds of its chiefs and warriors in epic cycles of poetry. By the 17th and 18th centuries this Gaelic tradition, although in decline, was kept alive by writers like Seathruin Ceitinn (Geoffrey Keating), who

cast sardonic and mournful censure on the oppression of English settlers and the passing of the old ways; but the Anglo-Irish tradition, as well as the Gaelic, could also be highly political and historical even in its earliest forms. The wit and satire of Swift's *The Story of the Injured Lady* and *The Modest Proposal*, and the unassuming but penetrating social novels of Maria Edgeworth, such as *Castle Rackrent* and *The Absentee*, are perhaps the best examples from before the famine. The list should also include Bishop Berkeley's probing social commentary in *The Querist*, and dramatists such as Richard Brinsley Sheridan and Oliver Goldsmith.

In the mid-19th century the most popular Irish writer was probably Thomas Moore (1779–1852), who became famous (and rich) by exploiting the commonly-held sentimental view of Ireland in his poems and songs — such as the 10-volume *Selection of Irish Melodies*. A more honest exponent of Irish traditional life was William Carleton (1794–1869), who was an acute observer of the peasant life from which he himself had come. His most famous works include *Traits and Stories of the Irish Peasantry* and the novel *Fardorougha the Miser*.

The most important development at this time came from Thomas Davis (1814–45) and the Young Ireland movement. Their work, published in the *Nation* and "The Library of Ireland," is rarely noteworthy for its artistic merit, but rather for creating an audience receptive to a "national" literature. In his ballads and verse such as *The Patriot Parliament of 1689* and *Lament for Eoghan Ruadh*

O'Neill, Davis expressed a romantic, patriotic and vigorous vision of 17th century Irish history which he hoped would inspire his present-day compatriots to break the Union. Eventually, interest grew in the ancient history and myth of Gaelic Ireland as well as the more recent past. The first important wave of interest in this material had come between 1760 and 1780, largely due to the somewhat dubious scholarship of James Macpherson and Charles Vallancey. But the key figure in the early stages of the latest Gaelic revival (which would come to full fruition in the 1890s) was Samuel Ferguson (1810–86). Ferguson was a Trinity College-educated antiquarian and poet from Belfast. His poems rediscovered many of the Celtic heroes — Cuchulain, Deirdre, Diarmid and Queen Maeve — that would become the stock-in-trade of later writers such as Yeats and Lady Gregory. The important Gaelic saga, the *Tain Bo Cuailgne* (The Cattle Raid of Cooley), was revived in Ferguson's *Lays of the Western Gael* (1864), and he wrote many prose tales based on Gaelic myths. These were collected posthumously by his wife, Lady Ferguson, in *Hibernian Nights' Entertainment* (1887).

However, according to Yeats, Standish O'Grady (1846–1928) was the father of the Celtic revival. O'Grady knew little Gaelic himself, and his *History of Ireland* (published in two volumes in 1878 and 1880) was not the first English translation of the Celtic sagas, but he made accessible the ancient myths and lore of the Celts to a much wider audience. He produced a string of works based on these myths over the next two decades, including *The Early Bardic Literature of Ireland* (1879), *Cuculain: An Epic* (1882), *Finn and his Companions* (1892) and *The Coming of Cuculain* (1894). Like Davis, he also drew extensively on 16th and 17th century themes. Somewhat ironically given O'Grady's Protestant ascendancy and elitist outlook, his work initiated the process whereby the emerging Catholic lower middle classes — shopkeepers, schoolmasters, publicans and clerks — began to associate nationalism with the heroics of ancient aristocratic Celtic heroes.

O'Grady's work also inspired Douglas Hyde and Eoin MacNeill to found the Gaelic League in 1893. Its aim was not only to revive and propagate the Irish language, but to encourage Irish writers to draw on their rich and ancient literary tradition. Many Gaelic Leaguers, notably Hyde, argued that Irish literature must be de-Anglicized (see Chapter 2), but the most remarkable aspect of the Celtic revival was the fusion of Anglo-Irish, Gaelic and European literary traditions in the writers associated with the Abbey Theatre — especially William Butler Yeats.

Yeats was born in Dublin in 1865 and spent many of his early years in London where his lawyer-turned-painter father had moved in 1867. Early influences include William Morris and the old Fenian John O'Leary — who thought there could be no great literature without nationality. The ardor of his youthful nationalism was no doubt heightened by his ardent love for the committed republican Maud Gonne, to whom he dedicated much early love poetry. Yeats was inspired by a wide range of eclectic, and often bizarre, interests. Theosophy, occultism and mysticism were influences as well as

ABOVE: Politics and art travel closely together in the century from 1845. This sculpture of the mythical Cuchulain in the GPO building on O'Connell Street is dedicated to the memory of those who fell in the 1916 Easter Rising.

BELOW: Patrick Pearse — Padraig MacPiaris — was both freedom fighter and poet. Executed in 1916 in the aftermath of the Easter Rising, he had been active in the Gaelic League and established a school for teaching the Irish language, St. Enda's College.

nationalism and, much later, a brief flirtation with fascism; but it was his growing interest in the Celtic revival that was most important in his early development. After forming an Irish Literary Society in London, he returned to Ireland in 1892 with the aim of creating a national literature based on folk tales and ancient Irish mythology. Using figures like Cathleen ni Houlihan and Cuchulain in both his poetry and in the plays, Yeats became the guiding light of the literary revival and one of the greatest poets of the modern era. In 1889 he published *The Wanderings of Oisin and other Poems*, and during the 1890s *The Countess Cathleen, The Secret Rose* and *The Wind Among the Reeds* followed. He then wrote plays for the Irish National Theatre Society — which had been founded by himself and fellow writers Lady Gregory, Edward Martyn and George Moore — most notably *On Baile's Strand, Deirdre,* and *Cathleen Ni Houlihan.* The latter, first produced in 1902, was perhaps the archetypal Nationalist play. Ireland herself is symbolized by an old woman (Cathleen) who persuades the young, vigorous Michael Gillane to leave his home, family and bride-to-be to sacrifice himself for the sake of Ireland. Fourteen years later, much to the surprise of Yeats, many young men followed Michael Gillane's example. Indeed some of the men who led the Easter Rising, including Pearse, Joseph Plunkett and Thomas MacDonagh, were themselves talented poets who had been inspired by Yeats' writings. Pearse and MacDonagh had even written their own plays intended for the Abbey Theatre. The line between art and politics was a fine one between 1900 and the 1920s.

All these writers drew on O'Grady's publication of

ABOVE LEFT: Eoin MacNeill was co-founder of the Gaelic League in 1893.

ABOVE: Maud Gonne, to whom Yeats dedicated so much of his early love poetry. She was a committed republican.

TOP: Born in Dublin in 1865, William Butler Yeats was the son of a celebrated painter. He studied at the School of Art in Dublin, working closely with George Russell ("AE"). A nationalist, he would serve as a senator of the Irish Free State 1922–28 and receive the Nobel Prize for Literature in 1923. He died in 1939 in the south of France but in 1948 his body was brought back to the area of his childhood, Drumcliff in Sligo.

ABOVE: John Millington Synge was born in 1871, educated at Trinity College, Dublin, but allegedly owes his fame to a meeting with Yeats in Paris in 1899 when the latter convinced him to use his talents to describe Irish peasant life — although he may well have been thinking along these lines already. This drawing is by Yeats's father, John, a talented artist.

RIGHT: Nobel Prize for Literature winner George Bernard Shaw did not spend much time in Ireland after 1876, pursuing his career as playwright and critic in London.

ancient Irish mythology, but much of their material came from the folklore of the common people, especially the poor Gaelic-speaking peasants of the west. Remote islands such as the Aran and then the Blasket islands were invaded by hordes of linguists and writers in search of authentic Gaelic speakers and folk stories for literary inspiration. The most important of these was probably John Millington Synge (1871–1909). Descended from an old aristocratic Anglo-Irish family, Synge spent time living among the people of the Aran islands, learning their ways and their language. He developed a deep affection for their noble and simple lives, which were barely touched by western civilization. These people, scratching out an existence from dangerous seas and rocky soils, still believed in fairies and magic, and were, he thought, unaffected by the greed, hypocrisy and social divisions which affected the rest of Ireland.

His experiences, which are told wonderfully in his *The Aran Islands*, provided the thematic material for most of his later work. As he states in the preface of his most famous, and most controversial play:

"... in writing *The Playboy of the Western World*, as in my other plays, I have used one or two words only, that I have not heard among the country people of Ireland ... and I am glad to acknowledge how much I owe to the folk imagination of these fine people."

He went on to explain why he used this source by comparing the fertility of the peasant mind with the sterility of modern urban life:

"In countries where the imagination of the people, and the language they use, is rich and living, it is possible for a writer to be rich and copious in his words, and at the same time give the reality which is the root of all poetry, in a comprehensive and natural form."

On the other hand the modern literature of towns dealt with "the reality of life in joyless and pallid words."

Synge's depiction of the western peasant was far from pleasing to everyone's taste. In *The Playboy* the two main characters are a young man who is on the run after he thinks he has killed his father, and a liberated, sexually confident woman called Pegeen Mike. This last character was too much for the sensitive urban tastes of bourgeois Dublin, who liked their stage peasants, especially their female stage peasants, to reflect a pure and virtuous Irish ideal. Portrayals of the peasantry were highly political (and often highly exploitative) in early 20th century Ireland. By portraying his peasants as real people with real passions and flaws, Synge effectively attacked the idea that art should be used for narrow nationalist ends.

This controversy affected Irish literature immensely from the turn of the century until independence. Yeats, Lady Gregory and Synge, while all broadly nationalist in sentiment (Yeats was a member of the Fenians and the IRB in his youth), demanded that art be allowed to express complex and personal realities and refused to accept that it should always be subservient to the

ABOVE: Oscar Wilde was born in Dublin in 1854, was educated in Enniskillen and Oxford and died in Paris in 1900. He spent his childhood at No. 1 Merrion Square, one of Dublin's largest and grandest Georgian squares. In the 1840s, during the famine, the square was used as a soup kitchen.

RIGHT: Trinty College, Dublin, has been the breeding ground for some of the greatest exponents of the English language — but few Catholics went there until the 1970s. It was founded as a Protestant college in 1592 by Queen Elizabeth I. Two statues flank the entrance, both sculpted by John Foley in the 1860s. This one is of Oliver Goldsmith; the other is of the political orator and statesman Edmund Burke.

nationalist struggle. By World War I Yeats had effectively turned his back on popular nationalism. His new dramas incorporated the symbolism of an esoteric new influence, Japanese Noh theater, and moved away from popular to private performance. Romantic Ireland, so it seemed, was dead and gone with O'Leary in the grave. However, the Easter Rising revived the patriotic side of his nature and inspired the famous poem, "Easter 1916." As Yeats put it, "All changed, changed utterly: A terrible beauty is born."

Two famous Irish writers who largely avoided nationalist issues by working in London were George Bernard Shaw and Oscar Wilde, but their writing nevertheless retained an Irish dimension. Wilde had been brought up in colorful circumstances in Dublin. His mother wrote nationalist prose under the pen name "Speranza," while his father was an eminent surgeon, notorious for his poor personal hygiene. As if to eradicate this almost comic, stage-Irish background he emigrated to England where he became more English than the English. In doing so he nevertheless ridiculed the manners of the English upper classes and hence retained a certain subversive Irishness. Wilde's novel *The Picture of Dorian Gray* (1890) is a powerful moral allegory which explores the excesses of the unrestricted libertinism of a certain kind of English gentleman, but his best works were for the stage. His unique combination of dazzling epigrammatic wit and rapier-like social satire can be found in *Lady Windermere's Fan*, *A Woman of no Importance*, *An Ideal Husband* and, especially, *The Importance of Being Earnest* — all of which were published between 1892 and 1895. Two more of his works should also be mentioned — the *Ballad of Reading Gaol* (1898), which represents Wilde's finest poetry, arose from his experiences there after his imprisonment for homosexual acts in 1895, and his short, passionate and brutal play, *Salome*, based on the death of John the Baptist. This was originally published in French in 1894, and is notable partly on its own merits and partly as the inspiration for one of the 20th century's greatest operas — *Salome* by Richard Strauss.

George Bernard Shaw (1856–1950) is now famous primarily for his witty political plays such as *Major Barbara*, *Pygmalion*, *Heartbreak House* and *Man and Superman*. In his own day he was a fine musical and theatrical critic. In addition he produced some brilliant polemical political writing which expressed advanced socialist and feminist views while rarely descending into dogma. As a satirist, intellectual, wit and dramatist, he stood like a colossus over the British literary scene from the late 19th century until World War II. He also maintained a keen interest in his native land, as evidenced by such works as *John Bull's Other Island* and *How to Settle the Irish Question*. However, he cannot really be classed as an Irish writer in the same sense as Yeats or Joyce.

James Joyce was another brilliant literary Irishman who also pursued his writing in self-imposed exile, but his subject matter marks him out as a distinctly Irish writer — despite his cosmopolitanism. Born in the south Dublin suburb of Rathgar in 1882, he was educated at Jesuit schools before studying modern languages at University

TOP: "AE" — George William Russell — became organizer of Sir Horace Plunkett's Agricultural Association in 1899 and helped found the Irish Agricultural Cooperative Movement. He was the editor of The Irish Statesman *from 1923 to 1930 and was called the "Sophocles of Dublin."*

ABOVE: No. 41 Brighton Square, where James Joyce lived before his self-imposed exile in Europe.

RIGHT: James Joyce was born in Dublin, educated in Dublin and wrote about Dublin extensively. All his best known works — Dubliners, Portrait of the Artist as a Young Man, Ulysses *and* Finnegan's Wake *— are set in Dublin, although he himself spent most of his last 35 years abroad.*

College, Dublin. Feeling dissatisfied with the restrictions of Irish life, he spent a year in Paris after graduating in 1902. On his return he received recognition and encouragement from Yeats and his circle, but after a brief sojourn in Ireland for his mother's funeral in 1903, he left Ireland again in late 1904. He spent most of the rest of his life, often in poverty, with his Irish partner Nora Barnacle (he eventually married her in 1931) until his death in Zurich in 1941.

This dissatisfaction with Ireland is expressed in *Dubliners* (a collection of short stories written between 1904 and 1907 but not published until 1914), and in the semi-autobiographical *Portrait of the Artist as a Young Man* (first serialized in *The Egoist* during 1914–15). In these works Joyce portrays Ireland as stagnant, dishonest, mercenary and parochial — a particularly unhealthy environment for a young inquiring artist. Religion especially was seen as a stultifying force — a "net" which could trap the artist. Yet, despite his wanderings in Europe, Joyce returned to Dublin in his writing, most notably in his most famous novel, *Ulysses*, first published in Paris in 1922. This vast work depicts a single day — June 16, 1904 — in the life of Leopold Bloom. It is consciously modelled on the epic wanderings of Homer's Odysseus — a man who spent two decades trying to find his way back to his rocky island homeland of Ithaca. Joyce's own lonely literary wanderings between Paris, Zurich and Trieste have an Odysseus-like flavor, but whereas Odysseus actually made it home in the end, Joyce only came home in his writing.

Among other things, *Ulysses* is a rejection of the Gaelic revival and a scathing critique of his fellow Irish writers. The work contains a set of often vicious and deeply unsympathetic parodies of contemporary Irish literary figures, as well as a highly critical literary history of Ireland. But Joyce's target is more than just Dublin or Ireland. The whole of western society, including its literature, takes on an oppressive force preventing the true freedom of Bloom and Dedalus. Joyce also pioneered the use of "stream of consciousness" in *Ulysses* and the work is widely regarded as one of the pinnacles of modernism, inspiring Auden and Ezra Pound among others. His reputation as one of the great modernists also rests on his last major work, *Finnegan's Wake*, which was first published complete in 1939 after appearing in parts as *Work in Progress* between 1928 and 1937.

Other pre-independence novelists who deserve mention are George Moore, and the co-authors Sommerville and Ross. Moore's novels, although also coming in for criticism from Joyce, often prefigure his own critical attitude to Irish traditions and mores. Moore's milieu was the country more than the city. In his novel *The Lake* (1905), and the short stories *The Untilled Field* (1903), organized Catholicism, poverty, emigration and a declining landlord class emerge as villains of rural Ireland. Moore, a Catholic who later converted to Protestantism and the son of an MP, was a well-established writer before his involvement in the Irish Literary Theatre and the cultural revival. Between 1880 and 1899 he lived mainly in London, producing a series of novels which included

A Drama in Muslin (1886) and *Esther Waters* (1894) — probably his best work. These works were influenced by European writers, especially Zola, as much as anything Irish. His contribution to the Abbey Theatre was huge, but after 12 years in Dublin a degree of disillusionment set in and he returned to London. His involvement in the cultural revival is retold in three volumes of memoirs, *Hail and Farewell*, which serve as an invaluable and entertaining history of the movement.

The partnership of Edith Sommerville and Violet Martin (Ross being a pseudonym) humorously caricatured the relationships between Anglo-Irish landlords and the "true" Irish on their estates. Their work can be a trifle elitist and patronizing, but their acute observations and brilliant comic writing are still worth reading. They produced a series of immensely popular novels and short stories, the best-known of which are *The Real Charlotte* (1894) and *Some Experiences of an Irish RM* (1899). Sommerville, who was also an accomplished artist and illustrator, continued writing after Martin's death in 1915, but her best work was in collaboration with her cousin.

After independence, Irish literature in Ireland continued to flourish. Yeats, who became a senator of the Free State, was still writing poetry and new talents such as Sean O'Casey had emerged. O'Casey's three most famous plays — *The Shadow of a Gunman* (1923), *Juno and the Paycock* (1924) and *The Plough and the Stars* (1926) — were all performed first at the Abbey. They are a classic example of the strong connections between politics and literature in Ireland. Mixing realism with expressionism, O'Casey explored the suffering brought by nationalism,

coercion and war to the lower classes in Dublin. In *The Shadow of a Gunman* the tragic consequences of small-scale IRA involvement and idle boasting during the War of Independence were brought into brutal focus amid the dismal setting of a Dublin tenement, while *The Plough and the Stars* was a de-glamorized view of the Easter Rising which provoked full-scale riots.

By the end of our period Ireland's most famous literary son was Samuel Beckett, who, like Joyce, spent much of his life outside Ireland in Paris. Although actively writing from the 1930s (his first book of verse, *Whoroscope*, was published in 1930 and his first novel, *Murphy*, in 1938) Beckett's reputation rests chiefly on works published in the 1950s and 1960s — notably his French novels *Molloy, Malone Meurt* and *L'Innommable*; and the English plays *Waiting for Godot, Endgame* and *Happy Days*. The plays established Beckett as the leading exponent of the theatre of the absurd, and he was awarded the Nobel Prize for Literature in 1966.

ABOVE LEFT: The Theatre Royal, Dublin, burned down in 1880: it would be replaced by the Abbey Theatre in 1904.

BELOW LEFT: Backstage at the Abbey Theatre in postwar years.

ABOVE: The Abbey Theatre was erected by A. E. Horniman of Manchester, a great admirer of Yeats, to provide a home for the National Theatre Company and as the primary public vehicle for the cultural revival. It opened in 1904 and saw many productions of plays — sometimes controversial — by Yeats, Synge and O'Casey.

Other 20th century Irish novelists and playwrights worthy of note include Frank O'Connor (1903–66), Flann O'Brien (1911–66) and Brendan Behan (1923–64). O'Connor was an excellent short story writer following in the tradition of Moore and Joyce. Yeats even went so far as to compare him to Chekov. O'Connor was persuaded by Yeats to write plays for the Abbey and then become its director. O'Brien's first novel, *At Swim-Two Birds* (1939),

ABOVE: Samuel Beckett was born in 1906, entered Trinty College in 1923, won the Nobel Prize for Literature in 1969 and died in 1980. Like Wilde he spent much of his life in France, many of his works being produced in French before translation into English.

RIGHT: Sean O'Casey was — according to himself — educated in the streets of Dublin. Born in 1884 at No. 85 Upper Dorset Street he would teach himself Irish, join the Gaelic League and IRB, and write about Dublin during the troubles. Critical attacks on his last play drove him to England from 1926.

also owes much to Joyce but remains a highly original, many-layered work. It depicts the legendary Finn MacCool as seen through the eyes of a Dublin student. O'Brien was also a brilliant journalist for the *Irish Times* from 1940 under the pseudonym "Myles na Gopaleen." Behan was born in a Dublin tenement and developed strong republican sympathies. After joining the IRA at the age of 14, he spent time in an English borstal and was convicted for carrying explosives in 1939. After deportation back to the Irish Free State, he was imprisoned for five years in 1942 for shooting an Irish policeman. It was while in prison that he began writing haunting nationalist poetry in Irish, and plays in stylized Dublin slang, which included *The Quare Fellow* (1954) and *The Hostage* (1958). His experiences in Borstal and in prison were recounted in his autobiography *Borstal Boy* (1958).

An Anglo-Irish tradition was continued in the 1930s and 1940s in the work of Elizabeth Bowen, who is best known for her short stories and novels such as *The Death of the Heart* (1938) and *The Heat of the Day* (1949). These love stories exhibit a sensitivity of characterization reminiscent of Henry James. Born in Dublin in 1899, she spent much of her life in London and died in 1973.

In the field of poetry, Yeats continued to dominate. He developed a rich, often pessimistic, lyricism in collections such as *The Tower* (1928) and *The Winding Stair* (1933). His last poems were dominated by the themes of "lust and rage" and he remained highly productive right up until his death in 1939, completing *Parnell's Funeral and Other Poems* in 1935, *New Poems* in 1938, and the posthumously-published *Last Poems and two Plays* in 1939.

Other talented poetic voices also emerged, however. From the north came Louis MacNiece (1907–63), a highly individual poet who often found Ireland an infuriating place. He, too, spent much of his life in England, where

he worked for the BBC from 1941 until his death, writing and producing radio plays such as *The Dark Tower* (1947). His poetry was often urban, but he also dealt in the eternal themes of love and loss, as well as an ambiguous sense of belonging to his native land. Among the radical, iconoclastic social realists of the young Dublin literary scene, Patrick Kavanagh (1904–67) stands out. Kavanagh was a poet who reacted against the romanticized image of the Irish peasantry often portrayed by Yeats and his followers. In his major work, *The Great Hunger* (1942), he gave a passionate and stark account of the suffering and poverty, both spiritual and material, of bachelor life in his native Monaghan. This controversial, blunt, anti-pastoral work evoked the same outraged emotions as Synge's "*Playboy*" and was even seized by the police.

Such treatment was not uncommon in Ireland and we must end our brief survey of Irish literature on a somewhat negative note. Until 1967, all Irish artists struggled with archaic and restrictive censorship laws which were vigilantly policed by the Catholic Church. Any work dealing with homosexuality, birth control or abortion was likely to be banned, as were explicit depictions of heterosexual relationships and all forms of pornography. Many works had to be smuggled in from the North or from Britain. One could argue that it was precisely such petty, restrictive attitudes which fired the imagination of writers like Joyce: there was even a belief in some circles that a certain kudos attached itself to censored works, thus inspiring new and avant-garde writing — the argument was that if a new work was not banned, it must be too conventional! This was clutching at straws: censorship was a serious blight on Irish cultural life. Somewhat strangely, Joyce's *Ulysses* was never officially proscribed. The 1927 censorship law required a complaint to be made before a work was banned and Joyce's stature must therefore have protected him. In Ireland, it seems, even the narrow-minded value their literary giants.

THE VISUAL ARTS

Attempts to create a national art did not succeed to the same degree as national literature. Few painters and sculptors took up Thomas Davis' entreaty to elevate the nationality of their compatriots — which even included suggestions for specific subject matter. Daniel Maclise probably came the nearest. *The Marriage of Princess Aoiffe of Leinster with Richard de Clare* was a huge historical canvas depicting a first, symbolic moment of union between the Anglo-Norman and Celtic worlds in 1170. Amid the carnage and grief of Waterford's fallen walls, Strongbow marries Diarmid MacMurrough's daughter and establishes a claim to the Kingdom of Leinster. However, Irish painters continued to be more cosmopolitan than patriotic in their themes and influences, and the most talented often pursued careers in Paris or London.

John Lavery (1856–1941) was probably the finest Irish portrait painter of his generation. He painted political portraits of Collins, de Valera and Redmond, spent most of his time in London, and was influenced by French Impressionism. Talented Irish landscape painters included Nathaniel Hone (1831–1917) and later Paul Henry (1876–1958). Walter Osborne (1859–1903) specialized in colorful coastal peasant communities to good effect, but could hardly be called nationalist. Jack B. Yeats is a partial exception to this rule. The brother of W. B. Yeats, he shared many of his patriotic and Gaelic preoccupations. In addition to his connections with the Gaelic revival through his brother, he developed a very fluid, individual style with bold use of color and overtly Gaelic themes. Their father, John Yeats, was also a distinguished painter, especially of portraits. In these he captured all the great literary figures of his day: Douglas Hyde, George Moore, Lady Gregory, "AE," John Synge and, of course, his own sons. The most memorable, if somewhat romantic, paintings to be inspired by the troubles came from Sean Keating, whose *Men of the South* and *Men of the West* provide enduring images of the conflict, especially the former with its depiction of a tense, but noble, flying column.

Architectural styles tended to follow English influence in the mid-19th century, and especially that of A. W. N. Pugin's Gothic Revival (see Chapter 6), but an interest in Hiberno-Romanesque churches flourished later in the century. The use of round towers, smooth pillars, interlaced decoration, and bold, round-headed doorways with chevron mouldings, gave a distinctly early medieval Irish feel to many late 19th and early 20th century

churches. St. Patrick's Church, Jordanstown, built by W. H. Lynn in the 1860s, is a good early example, but the style remained popular well into the 20th century and can be seen in the Ashlin memorial for Cardinal McCabe and J. J. McCarthy's chapel, both in Glasnevin cemetery.

Sculpture did not make a large impact of the Irish artistic scene in our period, except for statues and monuments erected to national heroes — the most memorable of which being Oliver Sheppard's *Cuchulain* in the General Post Office. However Celtic motifs, Shamrocks and harps have proliferated in the applied arts and crafts. Glass, furniture, jewellery, porcelain, books, clothing and all manner of carved wooden products all reflected the Gaelic revival from the 1890s onwards. The visual arts did not rival the brilliance of Ireland's literary culture, but they contributed to the creation of national identity.

MUSIC

The musical life of Ireland was divided between the music of the towns and the music of the country. The former was cosmopolitan and classical, and it tended to follow the fashions and trends of Britain and Europe. The latter was the native folk music of the Gaelic people, with its ballads, love songs, laments, and martial, humorous and drinking songs. It is this folk tradition which Ireland is most noted for, and rightly so, for traditional Irish folk music is among the richest and finest of any in the world. Played on instruments like fiddles, pipes, whistles, flutes, accordions and the *Bodhran* (a large flat, hand-held, hide drum), this music was passed down from generation to generation. It added life and color to fairs, and provided the essential ingredient for roadside dances in the summer months and house dances in the winter. The dance rhythms traditionally associated with Irish folk music were often a mixture of the imported and the native, with the jig, reel, and hornpipe owing something to Italy, Scotland and England respectively.

Both the famine and the decline in Gaelic had a serious impact on traditional Irish music from the mid-century onward. Ancient Gaelic lyrics lost their meaning for many, and this in turn made the music unpopular and alien in the predominantly English-speaking towns. The European-wide, romantic interest of musicians in their country's folk music, which inspired, for example, an

influential collection of German folk songs called *Des Knaben Wunderhorn* in 1804, was finally mirrored in the collection of Irish music from mid-century onward by antiquarians like George Petrie and his *Ancient Music of Ireland* (1855). But until the Gaelic revival of the 1880s this was hampered by a lack of knowledge of the Gaelic language, and so the music was often preserved without the words. This defect received a remedy of sorts in the work of Thomas Moore, who supplied his own romantic lyrics in English to Irish tunes, but these often bore little resemblance to the real Irish folk music.

By the 1880s Gaelic revivalists were taking their musical heritage seriously. The work of R. M. Levey and P. W. Joyce in the 1870s and 1880s did much to preserve ancient folksong and in 1888 Joyce published *Irish Music and Song* — the first collection of Irish folksong accompanied by the original Irish words. The turn of the century saw the foundation of two traditional Irish music festivals, the Feis Ceoli and An tOireachtas, and in 1904 the Irish Folk Song Society was founded with a journal to disseminate traditional music. These were important developments, but the spirit of Irish folk music needed interaction with everyday lives and concerns to survive. The literary nationalism of Thomas Davis and the other Young Ireland writers had given this new lease of life to traditional music. In their popular patriotic ballads we find the lyrical roots of the rebel songs of 20th century Irish folk music, which also draws on an older tradition of Gaelic laments and martial songs. Heightened political sentiments also led to the formation of pipe bands in the South, while Unionists in the North formed fife and drum bands which combined popular music with communal solidarity — often with Orange Order marches. This merging of the political and the traditional is seen in songs like Peadar Kearney's "A Soldier's Song" which became the Irish national anthem, and continues to this day in pubs and clubs in Ireland and all over the Irish diaspora.

Classical music also benefited from the natural musicality of the Irish people. Dublin had been a popular place for European performers and composers to visit since the 18th century, when Handel's great oratorio, the *Messiah*, was given its first performance there in 1741. Early in the 19th century Irish classical music-making

suffered a decline as fashionable society increasingly decamped to London after the Act of Union. Ireland's most famous classical musician of this period, the composer and pianist John Field, followed suit and spent much of his life abroad. During his sojourn in Russia he invented the nocturne, a form of piano music which would later be made famous by Chopin. Later in the century, Irish musical life revived. Dublin took its place on the international opera circuit, opera being by far the most popular form of musical entertainment in the city. Famous singers, like Swedish soprano Jenny Lind, played to packed houses of 3,800 in the Theatre Royal, Dublin, and in 1871 the Gaiety Theatre opened to put on the popular operettas of Offenbach and Gilbert and Sullivan. A succession of concert societies, such as the Ancient Concert Society, the Philharmonic Society and the Dublin Orchestral Society, put on a healthy number of performance each season in venues such as the Ancient Concert Rooms, and the two Anglican Cathedrals, St. Patrick's and Christchurch, continued to provide high-quality choral music. However, talented Irish-born composers and musicians continued emigrate to further their careers. Stanford became one of the leading late 19th century composers of choral music, but spent most of his adult life in England, while the popular opera composers Michael Balfe (1808–70) and Vincent Wallace (1812–65) became musical nomads in search of success. As a young man Balfe sang in the *Barber of Seville* in Paris before

producing his own operas in London, Paris, Berlin and St. Petersburg. Wallace had a particularly colorful life. Leaving Ireland at the age of 23, he traveled to Australia, was rescued from Maoris in New Zealand by a chief's daughter, narrowly escaped death at the hands of mutineers in the South Seas, and played for princes in India and Mexico before returning to London (via failed business ventures in America) to produce his opera *Maritana* to great acclaim while still in his early thirties! He achieved further success with *Lurline* while in Germany before retiring in broken health to the Mediterranean.

The best-known Irish classical performer of the 20th century was John McCormack (1884–1945), a tenor who achieved world renown without any formal musical education. He made his Covent Garden debut in 1907 and first performed at New York's Metropolitan Opera in 1909. He sang in opera houses all over Europe and especially in America, where he received citizenship in 1917. His performances of Rudolfo opposite Dame Nellie Melba in Puccini's *La Bohème* were among the most polished ever heard, but he retired from the operatic stage in 1923. His later career combined brilliant *Lieder* recitals with incredibly popular recordings of Irish melodies. He was made a papal count in 1928 for his sacred music, and his recording of Gounod's "Ave Maria" with Fritz Kreisler on the violin is legendary. He gave his farewell concert in Dublin 1938, and by the time of his death there in 1945 he had earned a lasting place in Irish affections.

RELIGION

PREVIOUS PAGE: Dressed up in their Sunday best, Innishmaan (the second of the Isles of Aran) islanders leave church. During the years 1841–71 the number of priests per lay person doubled, and church attendances grew.

ABOVE: St. Patrick — the patron saint of Ireland — at Faha on the Pilgrim's Route up Mt. Branden in Co. Kerry.

RIGHT: Emigrating Irishmen and women took their faith with them to the US as exemplified by St. Patrick's Cathedral in New York.

To say that religion has played a central role in Irish history would be something of an understatement. The intensity of both the devotion and division which religion has inspired has arguably shaped events in Ireland more than any other single factor. As a result, the brute facts of the English conquest, the Protestant Ascendancy, the struggle for independence and then partition, tend to focus discussions of religion in Ireland around the divisions between Catholic and Protestant. In its structure this chapter will follow those divisions, but in doing so it will also try to shed some light on the character of the different religious traditions in Ireland, not only to explain why they were so often at loggerheads with one another, but to reveal the values that profoundly influenced daily life.

CATHOLICISM

Religion, and especially Catholicism, was generally a source of comfortable continuity in Irish life. For many, a devout belief in God pervaded their lives: lives which were structured by the weekly ritual of mass, the local authority of the priest and the activities of the church in education, charity and health care. But the practice and power of Catholicism changed steadily after the famine. The authority of both the priest over his flock, and the bishops over the priesthood, undoubtedly increased (although they never became absolute). This was, in part, due to the influence of Cardinal Paul Cullen (1803–78). As Archbishop of Dublin from 1852 to 1878, and

Ireland's first cardinal from 1866, he ensured that the church became more organized, disciplined and "Roman" in its outlook. This trend had actually begun before the famine, but it became most evident in the second half of the 19th century. Attendance at mass increased dramatically, aided by a massive church-building program which provided more churches to attend.

The physical presence of these new churches was symbolic of the increasing prominence of the church in Irish life. In 1825 the Catholic St. Mary's Pro-Cathedral opened in Dublin, and the process was accelerated under Cullen. Neo-classical and, after mid-century more fashionable, Gothic Revival churches, sprang up all over Ireland. The architectural inspiration for much of this work came from the English Catholic convert Augustus Pugin (1812–52), who did some of his best work in Ireland — notably the cathedral in Killarney and St. Patrick's College, Maynooth. He also encouraged many others, such as J. J. McCarthy (1817–82), to continue in this style. McCarthy designed the chapel at Maynooth to complement Pugin's design and built fine cathedrals in Armagh, Thurles, Monaghan and Derry, as well as over 60 churches. Pugin's own son, who went into partnership with the Irishman George Ashlin, was also responsible for the ongoing late 19th century explosion of Catholic Gothic churches. Roughly speaking, the more prosperous and English-speaking Catholics (whether urban or rural) were more likely to attend these churches than the poorer Gaelic-speaking peasant, but the increase

ABOVE: *Connemara children following their confirmation.*

LEFT: *A well-attended funeral at St. Nicholas' church, Galway. Attendance rates at Irish churches were among the highest in Europe.*

RIGHT: *George's Church, Dublin.*

in formal worship was a general phenomenon. Reflecting this trend, the number of priests per lay person doubled between 1841 and 1871: from roughly one priest for every 3,000 parishioners, to a priest for every 1,500.

The changes in Catholic worship were qualitative as well as quantitative. Old practices which smacked of pagan Celtic customs were increasingly frowned upon.

Heavy drinking at patterns and wakes, and celebrations of the fertility of the land, were replaced by benedictions, rosaries, novenas, sober processions and a whole host of formal acts of worship and devotion. This entire process was further encouraged by the Vatican I council of 1870 (in which Cullen played a leading part). This reaffirmed the Pope's infallibility, much to the disgust of British and

ABOVE: Temple in the grounds of Allhallows College, Dublin.

Irish Protestants. It also sought to impose his authority (a position known as Ultramontanism) over the independence of Catholic churches within national borders (Gallicanism); but this attempt was never entirely successful in Ireland.

The Irish Catholic Church did not always follow the Vatican in political outlook. After the revolutions of 1848 (which saw a brief Roman Republic in the papal states) and the successful reunification of those Papal States with the rest of Italy in 1870, the Vatican became hostile to any form of radical or liberal politics. The general tendency in predominantly Catholic countries was for the church to ally itself with conservative elements within the state, but in Ireland this went against the grain — for it would effectively mean support for British rule in Ireland. Hence the church's involvement in politics was somewhat schizophrenic. Although, on the whole, it was often more liberal than might have been expected. In general the church supported Irish nationalism, but not of the violent persuasion. As in the populace at large, however, there was disagreement within the church about which forms of nationalist activity were compatible with Catholic teaching. Local priests (coming as they did from the same rural and trade backgrounds as their parishioners) often held similar nationalist views, and so many did lend their support to the Fenians and IRB.

Most notable among these was Fr. Patrick Lavelle, a fiery republican from county Mayo, who lambasted the landlord system in his book *The Irish Landlord Since the*

Revolution (1870) and gave encouragement to the Fenians in the *Catholic Doctrine of the Right of Revolution* (1862). He also performed the grave-side oration at the Fenians' public funeral for Terence Bellew MacManus, and he was accused of intimidation at the Galway election in 1872.

Lavelle's was a tradition which went back to Fr. John Murphy of 1798 fame and beyond: the local parish priest leading his flock against the injustice and tyranny of Protestant British rule — often with the disapproval of his more comfortable superiors divorced from the suffering of the poor. Lavelle's close association with revolutionary nationalism did indeed incur the wrath of Cullen, who sought to keep the priest out of politics unless he was simply defending the rights of the church or upholding Christian morality. But opinions were divided even in the hierarchy. Lavelle's own superior, Archbishop John MacHale of Tuam, defended him from Cullen, and MacHale himself supported the repeal of the Union in the 1840s and tenant rights in the 1850s. Cullen's distaste for Fenianism, however, does not imply pro-British sympathies. His refusal to attend levées at the Castle (formal audiences with the viceroy) and his dislike of the fashionable mid-century English converts to Catholicism (such as John Henry Newman) show his robust nationalist sentiments. The hierarchy as a whole may have officially condemned the Fenians and refused them the sacraments

ABOVE LEFT and RIGHT: The exposure of Parnell's relationship with Katherine O'Shea in the divorce courts finished Parnell's career, and while a coalition of interests toppled him, there is no doubt that the morality of the situation affected the Catholic laity.

BELOW: Letter to General Sir John Maxwell from Bishop O'Dwyer of Limerick, showing his response to the general's attempts to get him to remove priests sympathetic to the Easter Rising from office.

Ashford, Charleville, 17th May 1916

Sir,
I beg to acknowledge the receipt of your letter of 12th inst., which has been forwarded to me here. I have read carefully your allegations against [the two priests], *but do not see in them any justification for disciplinary action on my part. They are both excellent priests who hold strong national views, but I do not know that they have violated any law, civil or ecclesiastical. In your letter of 6th inst., you appeal to me to help you in the furtherance of your work as military dictator of Ireland. Even if action of that kind was not outside my province, the events of the past few weeks would make it impossible to have any part in proceedings which I regard as wantonly cruel and oppressive.*
You remember the Jameson Raid, when a number of buccaneers invaded a friendly State and fought the forces of the lawful government. If ever men deserved the supreme punishment it was they. But officially and unofficially, the influence of the British Government was used to save them, and it succeeded. You took care that no plea for mercy should interpose on behalf of the poor young fellows who surrendered to you in Dublin. The first information we got of their fate was the announcement that they had been shot in cold blood. Personally I regard your action with horror, and I believe that it has outraged the conscience of the country. Then the deporting by hundreds, and even thousands, of poor fellows without a trial of any kind seems to me to be an abuse of power, as fatuous as it is arbitrary, and altogether your régime has been one of the worst and blackest chapters in the history of the misgovernment of this country.

I have the honour to be, Sir
Your obedient servant,
Edward Thomas, Bishop of Limerick

(Bishop Moriarty of Kerry even went so far as to declare that hell was not hot enough nor eternity long enough for the Fenians), but Cullen was no "Castle Catholic."

Indeed the influence of the church within constitutional nationalist political organizations was important. Catholic priests were often the local leaders of O'Connell's campaigns, and priests continued to be active in nationalist politics up to the struggle for independence and beyond. Church support for the Home Rule Party was vital to its popularity, and withdrawal of that support could go a long way towards ensuring the destruction of individual or organizational popularity. The obvious example here is Parnell's fall after his affair with Katherine O'Shea became public — but we should not overstate the case. Nationalist legend paints the bishops as scheming villains bringing a great man down unjustly, but the bishops were only part of the coalition of interests which toppled Parnell: the British nonconformists who supported Gladstone's Liberals were arguably more important. Indeed, the bishops were initially reluctant to speak out on such a political issue while it looked as if the party and the nation would support Parnell. Hence, the church's influence over its flock was certainly strong, but usually only when it reinforced their own sentiments, and clerical interference in politics could provoke considerable anger, especially among advanced nationalists.

In the struggle for independence, the hierarchy faced particular problems, and generally felt obliged to condemn the shocking tactics of both sides. William Walsh, Archbishop of Dublin from 1885 to 1921, enjoyed a similar dominance in the church at this time as Cullen had, and faced similar problems with nationalists. He took a more diplomatic approach and consequently faced less personal hostility — for example, there was no official Catholic condemnation of the Easter Rising. By 1917 support for Sinn Fein, especially among the lower clergy, was commonplace, and in the 1916–22 period as a whole, many priests did become vocal in their condemnation of British coercion — most notably Bishop O'Dwyer of Limerick, a violent critic of the military authorities.

Culture and education, while still potentially political,

were often seen as safer arenas for the church to bring its influence to bear. Archbishop Croke of Cashel (who as a supporter of the Land League agitation was given a warning to scale down his political activities by Pope Leo XIII) became an important patron of the Gaelic Athletic Association in the 1880s and 1890s. He was rewarded with sporting immortality by the use of his name for Ireland's national stadium for Gaelic sports in Dublin. A number of priests were highly influential in the Gaelic League and the Gaelic language revival. Fr. Eugene O'Growney was one of the league's founders, and his *Easy Lessons in Irish* introduced Irish school children to Gaelic for decades. Fr. Peadar Ua Laoghaire was an important Gaelic scholar who did much to create a new Irish literature and promote Gaelic for everyday use (see Chapter 5), and Fr. Patrick Dineen was an eminent teacher, lexicographer and editor of ancient Gaelic texts.

This naturally leads to, arguably, the most important influence of the Catholic church on Ireland — its role in education. Ever since the illegal hedgerow schools run by Catholic priests in the 17th and 18th century, the church had shouldered the main burden of educating the Catholic population, although after the famine this was by choice rather than necessity. Reflecting the religious divisions in society at large, education became highly denominational, with the Catholic bishops rejecting any moves towards mixed schooling. Even when there were strong financial inducements to vest control of local schools in the government's Board of Commissioners, most chose to remain either partly or wholly outside the system. In Catholic areas the National School system (which had been launched in 1831) was usually managed by the clergy. These small, often single-teacher establishments with fewer than 50 pupils were the bedrock of primary education in Ireland. There were many schools outside this system, though. Girls' schools were often attached to convents, and boys came increasingly under the care of the Christian Brothers'. After their foundation in the early 19th century by Edmund Rice, the Christian Brothers' multiplied rapidly in mid-century even though the government refused to give them grants until much later. Secondary level schooling was patchy for much of the period, but provision was improved somewhat after 1878 when government grants were awarded on the basis of exam results. These usually went to religious schools as they tended to be the best organized at cramming their pupils, and so the church continued its control of education up to the threshold of college level.

University education was a different matter and the source of great controversy before 1908. The relaxation of the penal laws in the 1790s allowed Catholic seminaries, such as St Patrick's College, Carlow (1793) and Maynooth (1795) to open. For a time these provided

ABOVE: Gaelic sports revived in the 1880s and 1890s — here Hurling, as seen in the **Illustrated Sporting and Dramatic News** *of March 22, 1884.*

RIGHT: The Church played a significant part in the Land League. This is Archbishop Croke of Cashel, a patron of the league, who was also active on behalf of the Gaelic Athletic Association.

ABOVE: The Mission Settlement, Dugort, Achill Island was set up by an evangelizing body introduced to the island in 1834. By 1851 it had purchased the estate of the local landlord, Sir Richard O'Donnel. It soon established a church, schools, houses and a printing press mainly for the production of religious texts. The mission was responsible for raising the standard of living on the island through education and the introduction of farming methods. It was also responsible for sending many missionaries out from the islands.

TOP: Coming home from school.

RIGHT: Classroom on Achill in the 1930s.

ABOVE: The Queen's College (Ireland) Act of 1845 provided for the establishment by the government of colleges at Cork, Galway and Belfast, to provide higher education on a non-denominational basis. Queen's College Galway opened in 1849 and was mainly populated by Catholics. This picture is from the 1860/70s.

some lay education as well, but there was no proper university education available for Catholics in Ireland before the famine — Trinity College in Dublin, the only university in Ireland, being restricted to Protestants. This situation changed in 1845 with Peel's legislation for the establishment of the Queen's University with three provincial colleges. These secular colleges, based in Belfast, Cork and Galway, opened in 1849 and provoked outright opposition from the Catholic hierarchy at a national synod at Thurles (despite the sop of massively increased funding for Maynooth). In response the bishops planned their own Catholic University of Ireland, which opened its doors in 1854 in Dublin with John Newman as its first rector.

By the 1870s, the need for Catholics (and Protestant dissenters) to have their own state-funded denominational institutions was gradually becoming accepted. But Gladstone's compromise Education Bill (1873), which would have set up a number of essentially denominational colleges within the structure of a large, national, secular university based on the University of Dublin (ie. Trinity College), pleased no one. It was defeated narrowly in the Commons after opposition from the church and

the parliamentary party. Later that year religious tests for admission to Trinity College were abandoned by Act of Parliament, but it remained a symbol of Protestant privilege. In 1882, the continuing "ban" on Catholics attending the Queen's University in Ireland forced its dissolution. The 1884 Concordat between the Home Rule Party and Catholic bishops ensured that thenceforth Irish Party MPs would take the bishops' side on the university question, but it was not solved until 1908. In that year two technically non-denominational universities were set up each with its own religious flavour: these were the predominantly Protestant Queen's University, Belfast and the mainly Catholic National University of Ireland with colleges in Dublin, Cork and Galway.

This Catholic concern for denominational education was part of a broader social role for the church, which involved influence over the whole range of moral

behavior. A classic early example of this was the work of Fr. Theobald Mathew to reduce alcohol consumption. In partnership with the Quaker William Martin, he founded a total abstinence movement in 1838 to which three million had pledged themselves by its peak in 1842. Similar concerns went right through into the Free State era. From 1925 there was a church-inspired ban on divorce. This ban became formalized in the 1937 constitution, in which the church was given a powerful "special position" in the state. In 1930 the first Irish Censorship Board was established with strong clerical influence, and in 1935 the sale of contraceptives was made illegal. In both the 1947 and 1951 Health Acts much-needed provision for maternity health care had to be abandoned in the face of the church's disapproval. Their objections to the "mother-and-child" clauses were based on the grounds that state health care could be based on "totalitarian" rather than Catholic principles — although the church's fear that a UK-style national health service might interfere in their near-monopoly control of health care was also a factor.

This institutional power of Irish Catholicism was only one aspect of its importance in Irish life, and its spiritual role must not be forgotten. More than anything else,

ABOVE: The Orangemen march — the more Home Rule became associated with Catholicism, the more it lost support among Protestants. Economics also divided Ulster from the rest of Ireland: it had gained prosperity under the Union and both workers and business leaders alike saw the link as vital to their continued success. The result was polariazation and the seeds of future conflict.

Catholicism provided an often impoverished people with both psychological security and a focus for their deep spirituality: a spirituality intensified by economic conditions which, for many, necessarily transferred hopes of comfort and happiness from this world into the next.

Prayers to the saints for intercession on their behalf and an almost obsessive devotion to Mary preserved a hint of pre-Christian paganism in Irish Catholicism which survives to this day and continues to baffle Protestants. The sincere devotion of Catholic belief in Ireland could not be doubted. Of course, over the duration of our period, Irish Catholicism moved steadily away from the open-air masses for the peasantry of the pre-famine days, and by the turn of the century there were plenty of comfortable, well-dressed, middle-class Catholics whose spirituality consisted of no more than a respectable weekly promenade to their grand new church. But Catholicism still provided the opium of the masses, and religious belief was the defining feature of many Irish lives, rich and poor.

PROTESTANTISM

The 1861 census revealed something that had been known for a long time: Irish Protestants were in a minority. They accounted for only about 22 percent of the population. This proportion increased slightly as the overall Irish population fell through predominantly Catholic emigration, but the religious split in Ireland remained roughly three-quarters Catholic and one-quarter Protestant throughout our period. The two main Protestant groupings were the Church of Ireland and the Presbyterians. There were a number of other small Protestant churches, but the only one of any size was the Methodists and they never accounted for more than 1.5 percent of the populace. The vast majority of Protestants lived in Ulster, which had a 50:50 Catholic-Protestant split in 1861, but they were also spread throughout the country, often forming large minorities in the towns. Of the remaining three provinces, Leinster, in particular, had a significant Protestant minority of 14 percent, many of whom were concentrated in Dublin, which had been a predominantly Protestant city in the 18th century. Although the Anglican and Presbyterian communities have very different historical and psychological roots, over the course of the 19th century their political and social differences narrowed in the face of the perceived Catholic nationalist threat. Thus we need to examine these different roots before explaining their political alliance in Unionism, and especially Ulster Unionism.

The Protestant Church of Ireland was essentially the religion of the English settlers transplanted to Ireland in the 16th and 17th centuries. Its origins lie in the English Reformation of Henry VIII and the resulting Church of England, which was then brought to Ireland by the Tudor conquerors. Hence the Church of Ireland's adherents are often referred to as "Anglicans" due to their similarities in doctrine and organization with the Church of England. Indeed, throughout its history, English and Irish clerics have frequently passed from one church to the other. This allowed English bishops to maintain control of the Irish church and provided a convenient exile for out of favor clerics such as Dean Swift.

The wars of the 17th century established the Church of Ireland as the legally sanctioned form of worship in Ireland, despite its minority status, and throughout the 18th century its practitioners were the dominant political and economic force in the land. The penal laws of the Anglican parliament in Dublin discriminated against both Catholics and Presbyterians, and led Anglicans to assume that privilege and power were their birthright. The Sacramental Test Act refused non-Anglicans admission to senior government, military, judicial and educational office, while the Corporation Act debarred them from local government. This led to great resentment on the part of the Presbyterians, which was, in turn, reinforced on the Anglican side by the Presbyterian connection with radical politics. Radical criticisms of the Protestant Ascendancy, and especially ones which called for an alliance of all faiths to achieve reform in the 1790s, were felt to be dangerous to the stability of a state with such a large Catholic majority. This mutual suspicion lasted deep into the 19th century, and to some extent persists today.

The traditional image of Anglicanism as the religion of the Protestant Ascendancy can obscure the fact that there were considerable numbers of working-class Anglicans, especially in Dublin and Belfast, as well as many ordinary farmers who adhered to the Church of Ireland. Yet Anglicanism was the religion of the landed gentry and the professions and, as such, it continued to enjoy great prestige and power until shortly before independence. By 1881, there were 636,000 Anglicans in Ireland (around 12 percent of the population) and many of these still dominated the army, the grand juries, city corporations, the top legal positions and most other official functions.

Throughout the second half of the 19th century, however, the church's position of privilege and power was gradually being chipped away. The church had actually been under attack since before the famine, with a violent campaign against the long-standing injustice of Catholics (and Dissenters) having to pay tithes to maintain an alien religious establishment. This campaign led to the first concrete signs of the church's diminished status — the 1833 Church Temporalities Act, which abolished 10 out of 22 bishoprics and scaled back the church establishment. The defining moment of the century for the Church of Ireland was the act for its disestablishment in 1869. After its implementation in 1871, Anglicans enjoyed virtually no formal political or economic benefits from their religion, although the Church of Ireland received a generous settlement and continued to be a wealthy institution.

By the first decade of the 20th century the ideological and spiritual leadership of Irish Protestantism was shared (and perhaps dominated) by the Presbyterian Dissenters. Although slightly smaller in number (around 10 percent of the population), they were more concentrated in Ulster and had grown increasingly prosperous through its industries and trade. The Presbyterian dissenting tradition had usually been particularly hostile to Catholicism (or "Popery" as it liked to call it). The deeply independent and Calvinistic spirit of its theology was seen as totally incompatible with the hierarchical and doctrinal authority of the Catholic Church (and for that matter, the episcopal authority of the Church of Ireland). Thus most Presbyterians, like many Anglicans, were afraid of the influence of a Catholic majority on a self-governing Ireland. They thought Home Rule would become Rome Rule, and while this fear seems exaggerated and melodramatic in the early 20th century, there was enough evidence of the power of the Catholic hierarchy to make it plausible to those already steeped in historical mistrust of popery. In fact they had the same set of prejudices as their 17th century ancestors, who had arrived in Ulster from Scotland determined to protect their freedom of worship from the persecuting spirit of Catholicism.

RIGHT: Belfast's Alfred Street Presbyterian Church. By the 1910s the spiritual leadership of Irish Protestantism was dominated by the Presbyterian Dissenters in the north.

This independence of spirit, as well as prompting further emigration to America (where they became known as the Scots-Irish), also saw a constant succession of splits and secessions. The main division was between those who would and those who would not subscribe to the 39 Articles of Faith contained in the Westminster Confession. Most did subscribe, and as these articles were also the basis of the Church of Ireland's doctrine, this gave them a basic community of belief with their fellow Protestants. But the dislike of externally imposed doctrinal authority was a constant feature of Irish Presbyterianism, which always preferred to take its lead from the Bible rather than doctrines agreed by synods of clerics. The 1830s, in particular, were a difficult time for Presbyterians as non-subscribers withdrew from the Synod of Ulster to form the Association of Non-subscribing Presbyterians, while in 1836 that other bastion of Protestant life, the Grand Orange Lodge of Ireland, dissolved after criticism in parliamentary reports. However, by 1840 Henry Cooke had reunited many Presbyterians in a new General Assembly and set the pattern of Anglican-Presbyterian co-operation to protect the Union. In the face of O'Connellite Catholic nationalism, it was increasingly felt that Union must be protected.

In the late 1850s both Protestant sects, but especially the Presbyterians, had been inspired by a great wave of emotional religious revival. Near-hysterical preachers like "Roaring" Hugh Hanna worked their audiences into a state of frenzy or ecstasy and often combined their religious message with a political one (although the two can hardly be separated in Ulster). The consequences were bloody rioting in Belfast in 1857 and a hardening of

ABOVE: Dublin Castle's Church of the Holy Trinity next to the 1258 Record Tower. The church was completed in 1814 and decorated by Edward Smyth.

RIGHT: The elaborately carved tomb of the powerful Boyle family in St. Patrick's Cathedral was carved in 1632; the flags above are of the Connacht Rangers.

FOLLOWING PAGE: Dublin children play in the street in the 1940s.

Protestant support for the Union as guarantor of their faith. Through the reconstituted Orange Order Protestants united in defence of the Union, and from the 1880s historians can talk of a united Protestant opposition to Home Rule. In the Solemn League and Covenant of 1912 (see Chapter 2) the fusion of the political and religious in a quasi-spiritual appeal to God for the protection of his chosen people can be seen. The Ulster Protestants could not prevent an independent south, but they stood firm in refusing to become part of it and received their own state in the six counties of Ulster in 1920. The presence of a large Catholic "fifth column" in this state encouraged further co-operation between Protestants, and 1923 witnessed the first meeting of United Council of Christian Churches and Religious Communions (consisting of the Church of Ireland, the Presbyterians and the Methodists). At the very end of our period, the dissenting tradition of splinter sects and violent anti-Catholicism was still very much alive — as the foundation of Ian Paisley's Free Presbyterian Church in 1951 testifies.

CHRONOLOGIES

POLITICAL

1845   Queen's College's Act passed (July 31)
First signs of potato blight appear (Sept)
Thomas Davis dies in Dublin (Sept. 16)

1846   Repeal of Corn Laws by Peel (June 26)
New Whig government under Lord John Russell replaces Peel (June 30)
Split between O'Connell and Young Ireland over use of violence (July)
Potato crop fails completely (Aug.–Sept.) — government does not intervene

1847   Foundation of Irish Convention by Young Irelanders (Jan. 13)
Height of famine — soup kitchens established (Feb.)
Daniel O'Connell dies in Genoa, Italy (May 15)
Poor Relief Act establishing outdoor (ie. not workhouse) relief (June)
Potato crop healthy but small (Aug.)

1848   John Mitchel founds radical newspaper, the *United Irishman* (Feb.)
Mitchel convicted and transported under the Treason-Felony Act (May)
Unsuccessful Young Ireland rising at Ballingary, Co. Tipperary (July)
O'Brien, Meagher and MacManus convicted of high treason (Oct.); death sentences commuted to transportation for life in June 1849

1849   Potato blight returns (May), crop fails again (Aug.)
Encumbered Estates Act helps indebted landlords sell land (July 28)
Queen's Colleges in Belfast, Cork and Galway open (Oct.)

1850   Irish Tenant League Founded (Aug. 9)
Irish Reform Act increases county but reduces borough voters (Aug. 14)

1852   First St. Patrick's Day march in New York (March 17)
Tenant League Conference in Dublin (Sept.)

1854   Catholic University opens in Dublin (Nov. 3)

1855   Emmet Monument Association founded in New York (Feb.)

1856   Phoenix Society founded at Skibbereen, Co. Cork by O'Donovan Rossa

1858   Irish Republican Brotherhood founded in Dublin by James Stephens (March)

1859   Fenians founded in New York by John O'Mahony (April)

1862   Harland & Wolff started in Belfast (Jan. 1)

1866   Fenian "invasions" of Canada (April–June)
Archbishop Cullen of Dublin becomes Ireland's first Cardinal (June)

1867   Attempted Fenian Rising in Ireland and England (Feb.–March)
Clan na Gael established in New York (June)
Sgt. Brett killed as Kelly and Deasy are rescued in Manchester (Sept. 18) "Manchester Martyrs" Allen, Larkin and O'Brien executed (Nov. 23)
Fenian explosion at Clerkenwell Prison (Dec. 13)

1868   Irish Reform Act reduces borough property qualification to £4 (July)

1869   Amnesty Association for the release of Fenian prisoners founded (June)
Irish Church Act disestablishes the Church of Ireland (July 26)

1870   Gladstone's first Land Act recognizes principle of Tenant Right (Aug. 1)
Isaac Butt founds the Home Government Association (Sept.)

1871   Disestablishment of Church of Ireland takes effect (Jan. 1)
Fenian Invasion of Canada (Oct. 5)

1873   The Home Rule League established (Nov.)

1874   59 Home Rule MPs elected — Gladstone replaced by Disraeli (Feb.)

1876   IRB and Clan na nGael form revolutionary directory and disown Home Rule

1877   Home Rule MPs Biggar, Parnell and O'Donnell adopt policy of obstruction
Parnell president of the Home Rule Confederation of Great Britain (Aug.)

1878   "New Departure" sees Fenian co-operation with Home Rule Party (Oct.)

1879   IRB Supreme Council rejects "New Departure" of Davitt and Devoy (Jan.)
Irishtown meeting (April 20)
Isaac Butt dies (May 5)
Land War begins after three successive bad harvests
Foundation of Irish National Land League (Oct. 21)

1880   Parnell tours US and addresses House of Representatives (Jan.–March)
General Election returns Gladstone's Liberals to power
Parnell elected chairman of the Irish Parliamentary Party (May 17)

1881   Ladies' Land League established
Gladstone's second Land Act — rents fixed by Land Commission Court (Aug.)
Parnell and other leaders arrested, Land League outlawed (Oct.).
No Rent Manifesto issued by imprisoned Land League leaders

1882   "Kilmainham Treaty" — Parnell released from prison (May 2)
Cavendish and Burke murdered by Invincibles in Phoenix Park (May 6)
Crime Prevention Act in response to Phoenix Park murders (July 12)
Irish National League takes over from banned Land League (Oct. 17)

1884   Catholic bishops and Home Rule Party agree on Catholic education (Oct. 1)
Gaelic Athletic Association founded by Michael Cusack (Nov. 1)
Franchise Act gives vote to every household (Dec. 6)

1885   Ashbourne Land Act accelerates purchase of farms by tenants (Aug. 14)
Home Rule party win 85 seats and hold balance of

power (Nov.–Dec.)

Gladstone converted to Home Rule (Dec. 17)

1886 Gladstone's first Home Rule Bill is defeated in the Commons (June 8)

Split in Liberal Party — Gladstone defeated in General election (July)

Serious sectarian rioting in Belfast (June–Sept.)

"Plan of Campaign" to withhold rents begins (Oct.)

1887 A letter in the *Times* links Parnell to Phoenix Park murders (April)

1888 Special Commission appointed to investigate the *Times'* accusations (Aug.)

1889 Special Commission reveals Pigott as forger of the *Times'* letter (Feb.)

Capt. O'Shea names Parnell as co-respondent in divorce case (Dec. 24)

1890 O'Shea's divorce suit hearing decides against Parnell (Nov. 17)

Gladstone's letter urging Parnell's resignation published (Nov. 25)

Majority of Home Rule Party and Catholic hierarchy denounce Parnell — Home Rule Party splits (Dec.)

1891 Balfour Act extends land purchase and sets up Congested Districts Board

Parnell marries Katherine O'Shea (June 25)

Parnell dies in Brighton (Oct. 6)

1893 Gaelic League founded by Douglas Hyde and Eoin MacNeill (July 31)

Second Home Rule Bill passes Commons but defeated in the Lords (Sept.)

1894 Gladstone resigns as PM (March 3)

Horace Plunkett founds Irish Agricultural Organization Society (April)

Irish Trades Union Congress established (April)

1895 Liberal party replaced by Salisbury and the Conservatives.

1896 James Connolly founds the Irish Socialist Republican Party (May 29)

1898 United Irish League founded by William O'Brien (Jan. 23)

Ancient Order of Hibernians revived in US (June)

Local Government Act greatly extends franchise and includes women (Aug.)

1899 Department of Agriculture and Technical Instruction established (Aug. 9)

1900 Home Rule Party reunites under leadership of John Redmond (Jan. 30)

Arthur Griffith founds Cumann na nGaedheal (Sept. 30)

1902 Land Conference of landlords and nationalists, Dunraven in Chair (Dec.)

1903 Wyndham Land Act (based on Land Conference report) (Aug. 14)

1904 Pro-devolution Irish Reform Association established by Dunraven (Aug.)

1905 First Dungannon Club formed by Bulmer Hobson (March 8)

Ulster Unionist Council founded (March)

1906 Landslide victory for the Liberals in General Election (Jan.)

1907 Sinn Fein formed from Cumann na nGaedheal and

Dungannon Clubs (April 21)

Larkin's dock strike in Belfast — rioting and police mutiny (May–July)

Devolutionary Irish Council Bill abandoned by Liberals (June)

1908 Irish Universities Act (Aug. 1)

Old Age Pensions Act (Aug. 1)

Irish Transport Workers' Union (later ITGWU) founded by Larkin (Dec. 29)

1909 Fianna Eireann founded by Bulmer Hobson and Countess Markievicz (Aug.)

Lloyd George's radical "People's Budget" rejected by the Lords

Birrell's Land Act introduces compulsory land purchase (Dec. 3)

1910 General Election gives Home Rule Party the balance of power (Jan.)

William O'Brien founds the All-for-Ireland League

1911 Parliament Act restricts Lord's veto on legislation to two years (Aug.)

1912–23 (See separate chronology on pages 188–89)

1923 Irish Free State becomes a member of the League of Nations (Sept. 10)

1924 National Army reorganization leads to "mutiny"

1925 Boundary Commission abandoned, existing partition accepted Dec. 3)

Northern Nationalists take their seats in Northern Ireland Commons

1926 De Valera founds Fianna Fail (May 16)

1927 Agricultural Credit Corp established (May 28)

Kevin O'Higgins killed — Public Safety and Constitution Bills (July)

De Valera and Fianna Fail enter Dail (Aug.) after election (June)

1929 Censorship of Publications Act in Irish Free State (July 16)

Proportional representation ended in NI elections (April 16)

1931 IRA banned in the Irish Free State

Statute of Westminster gives law-making independence to dominions (Dec.)

1932 Army Comrades Association (later known as Blueshirts) formed (Feb. 9)

Fianna Fail win general election, de Valera leads government (March)

Withholding of land annuities leads to Tariff War with UK (July)

Riots and strikes in Belfast over unemployment (Oct.)

Formal opening of NI parliament building at Stormont (Nov. 16)

1933 National Guard formed from Blueshirts with Gen. O'Duffy as leader (July)

National Guard (Blueshirts) banned (Aug. 22)

Fine Gael formed from Cumann na nGaedheal and National Guard (Sept.)

1934 O'Duffy is replaced by Cosgrave as Fine Gael leader (Sept.)

Anglo-Irish Coal-Cattle Pact (Dec. 21)

1935 Contraceptives banned in Irish Free State

1936 IRA declared illegal by de Valera's government (June 18)

Amending Act ends internal role of Crown and

Governor-General (Dec. 11)

External Relations Act limits Crown to foreign relations (Dec. 12)

1937 New constitution approved — Irish Free State becomes Eire (June)

1938 Anglo-Irish agreement to end Tariff War — treaty ports returned (April)

NI welfare state brought into line with UK

1939 IRA bombing campaign in Britain (Jan.–Aug.)

World War II begins — Eire declares neutrality (Sept.)

1940 Emergency Legislation against IRA in Eire (Jan.)

Anglo-Irish military consultations

Prime Minister of NI, Viscount Craigavon (James Craig) dies (Nov. 24)

1941 German air raids on Belfast (April) and parts of Eire (Jan. and May)

1943 Sir Basil Brooke becomes Prime Minister of Northern Ireland (April 28)

1944 Split in Irish Labour Party (Jan.)

1945 De Valera expresses formal condolences on death of Hitler (May 2).

World War II ends in Europe (May 8)

Churchill's victory speech critical of Ireland — de Valera's reply (May)

1946 Clann na Poblachta founded under leadership of Sean MacBride (July 6)

1947 Universal secondary education in Northern Ireland

1948 General Election — Costello leads Fine Gael coalition government (Feb.)

National Health Service introduced to NI (Feb. 4)

Republic of Ireland Act repeals External Relations Act of 1936 (Dec. 21)

1949 Eire formally declared the Irish Republic (April 18)

Ireland Act in UK guarantees continuance of Northern Ireland (June 2)

THE PATH TO REVOLUTION

1912

9 April   Conservative leader Bonar Law pledges support for Ulster Unionists

11 April   Third Home Rule Bill introduced by Asquith

28 Sept.   450,000 sign the Solemn League and Covenant in Ulster

1913

30 Jan.   Home Rule Bill is defeated in Lords

31 Jan.   Ulster Volunteer Force established

15 July   Second defeat of Home Rule Bill in Lords

26 Aug.   Strike of ITGWU led by Larkin begins

2 Sept.   Employers lock-out of strikers, led by William Martin Murphy, begins

19 Nov.   Irish Citizen Army founded

25 Nov.   Irish Volunteers founded

1914

20 March   The Curragh "Mutiny"

24 April   Gun-running of Ulster Volunteers at Larne, Bangor and Donaghadee

25 May   Home Rule Bill passes Commons for the third and final time

21 July   Buckingham Palace Conference to negotiate future of Ulster opens

26 July   Howth gun-running by Irish Volunteers, soldiers kill four in crowd

4 Aug.   Britain declares war on Germany after invasion of Belgium

18 Sept.   Home Rule Bill given royal assent but suspended until end of war

20 Sept.   Redmond's Woodenbridge speech commits Irish Volunteers to war effort

24 Sept.   Irish Volunteers split over Redmond's speech

1915

25 May   Wartime coalition cabinet of Lloyd George with Carson and Bonar Law

29 July   Funeral of O'Donovan Rossa; Pearse's funeral oration

Dec.   IRB Military Council begins Easter Rising plans

1916

21 April   The *Aud* captured in Tralee Bay with German arms for rising

22 April   Maneuvers of Volunteers planned for next day cancelled by MacNeill

24 April   Easter Rising by Volunteers and Citizen Army in central Dublin

29 April   Pearse orders insurgents to surrender

3–12 May   Execution of 15 leaders of the rising, including Pearse and Connolly

1917

5 Feb.   First Sinn Fein election victory — Count Plunkett at Roscommon.

10 July   De Valera wins East Clare by-election for Sinn Fein

25 Oct.   De Valera elected President of Sinn Fein

1918

5 April   Irish Convention fails in to reach compromise

18 April   Military Service Act gives power to impose conscription in Ireland

17 May   "German Plot" arrests of Sinn Fein leaders

Dec.   Sinn Fein landslide in General Election — 73 of 105 Irish seats

1919

21 Jan.   War of Independence begins — two RIC policemen killed at Soloheadbeg

21 Jan.   First meeting of Dail Eireann makes declaration of independence

1 April   De Valera elected President of the Dail Eireann

11 June   De Valera arrives in US for 18-month fund-raising tour

20 Aug. Volunteers (IRA) swear allegiance to the Republic and the Dail

12 Sept. British government declares Dail Eireann illegal

1920

2 Jan. Black and Tans formed

15 Jan. Sinn Fein wins control of 172 of 206 local councils

23 May Railway workers strike and refuse to carry troops

July–Aug. Riots in Belfast lead to 30 deaths — Catholics driven from shipyards

27 July RIC Auxiliaries formed from ex-army officers

20 Sept. Raid on Balbriggan by Black and Tans

25 Oct. Terence MacSweeny, mayor of Cork, dies in prison on hunger strike

1 Nov. Execution of Kevin Barry

21 Nov. "Bloody Sunday" — 14 British agents shot, 12 killed in Croke Park

11 Dec. Cork city sacked and burnt by Black and Tans

23 Dec. Government of Ireland Act establishes Northern Ireland parliament

1921

4 Feb. Sir James Craig replaces Sir Edward Carson as Ulster Unionist leader

25 May IRA attack and burn Dublin's Custom House

7 June Northern Ireland parliament opens — Craig first prime minister of NI

22 June At official opening of NI Parliament, George V calls for peace

9 July Truce agreed between IRA and British army

11 Oct. Peace Conference opens in London

6 Dec. Anglo-Irish Treaty signed, leading to split in Sinn Fein and IRA

1922

7 Jan. Treaty accepted by Dail by 64 votes to 57 — with de Valera opposing

9 Jan. Arthur Griffith becomes president, defeating de Valera by two votes

16 Jan. Provisional government, with Collins as head, takes over power

Feb–May Serious sectarian violence in Belfast

7 April Special Powers Act in NI

April Anti-Treaty IRA seize Four Courts in Dublin and other strongholds

16 June Pro-treaty parties win large majority in first Free State elections

22 June Field Marshal Sir Henry Wilson killed in London by IRA

28 June Government attack on anti-treaty IRA in Four Courts starts Civil War

12 Aug. Arthur Griffith dies

22 Aug. Michael Collins killed in an ambush at Bealnablath, Co. Cork

9 Sept. Third Dail Eireann elects William T. Cosgrave as President

25 Oct. Constitution of Irish Free State approved by Dail

17 Nov. Erskine Childers the first of 77 government executions of republicans

1923

March Cosgrave founds Cumann na nGaedheal from pro-Treaty Sinn Fein

27 April Anti-Treaty forces in Civil War end fighting (May)

ARTS & LITERATURE

1842 First number of the *Nation* (Oct. 15)

1854 Oscar Wilde born in Dublin
Act for Establishing a National Gallery in Ireland (Aug. 10)

1856 George Bernard Shaw born in Dublin

1860 William Carleton's *Collected Works* published

1865 William Butler Yeats born in Dublin

1870 Charles Kickham's *Knocknagow* begins serialization in *Emerald* and *Shamrock*

1871 Gaiety Theatre opens in Dublin

1873 *Knocknagow* published complete in Dublin (June)

1878–81 Standish O'Grady's *History of Ireland: Heroic Period*

1882 James Joyce born in Dublin

1884 Gaelic Athletic Association established by Michael Cusack (Nov. 1)

1888 P.W. Joyce's *Irish Music and Song* published

1890 National Library and Science & Art Museum open in Dublin (Aug. 29)
Wilde's *The Picture of Dorian Gray*

1892 Douglas Hyde's *On the Necessity for De-Anglicizing the Irish People*

1893 Gaelic League established by Hyde and MacNeill (July 31)

W. B. Yeats's *The Celtic Twilight*

1894 Oscar Wilde's *Salome*
George Moore's *Esther Waters*

1895 Wilde's *The Importance of Being Earnest* and *An Ideal Husband*

1898 Oscar Wilde's *The Ballad of Reading Gaol*

1899 First number of the Gaelic League's *An Claidheamh Soluis* (March 18)
W. B. Yeats's *The Countess Kathleen* opens the Irish Literary Theatre (May 8)

1900 Geoffrey Keating's *Poems* — first publication of the Irish Texts Society
Oscar Wilde dies in Paris

1901 Douglas Hyde's *Casadh an tSugain* — the first modern play in Irish

1902 W. B. Yeats's *Cathleen ni Houlihan* first performed (April 2)
Ulster branch of Irish Literary Theatre founded (Nov.)

1903 Irish Literary Theatre renamed Irish National Theatre (Feb. 1)
J. M. Synge's *In the Shadow of the Glen*
Lady Augusta Gregory's *Poets and Dreamers*

George Moore's *The Untilled Field*

1904 George Bernard Shaw's *John Bull's Other Island*
Foundation of Irish Folk Song Society
J. M. Synge's *Riders to the Sea*
The Abbey Theatre opens (Dec. 27) with Yeats's *On Baile's Strand* and Lady Gregory's *Spreading the News*

1905 G. B. Shaw's *Man and Superman* and *Major Barbara*
J. M. Synge's *The Well of the Saints* performed at the Abbey

1906 Samuel Beckett born

1907 J. M. Synge's *The Playboy of the Western World* causes riots at the Abbey
J. M. Synge's *The Aran Islands*
Lady Gregory's *The Rising of the Moon* performed at the Abbey

1909 J. M. Synge dies of Hodgkinson's disease
John McCormack makes his debut at the New York Metropolitan Opera House

1911–13 George Moore's *Hail and Farewell*

1913 G. B. Shaw's *Pygmalion*

1914 James Joyce's *Dubliners* published (written in 1904)

1916 James Joyce's *Portrait of the Artist as a Young Man* published

1920 G. B. Shaw's *Heartbreak House*

1922 James Joyce's *Ulysses* published in Paris

1923 W .B. Yeats awarded Nobel Prize for Literature
G. B. Shaw's *Saint Joan*
Sean O'Casey's *The Shadow of a Gunman* performed at the Abbey

1924 Sean O'Casey's *Juno and the Paycock* performed at the Abbey

1925 G. B. Shaw awarded Nobel Prize for Literature

1926 Sean O'Casey's *The Plough and the Stars* opens at the Abbey

1928 John McCormack made a Papal Count

1929 Censorship of Publications Act in Irish Free State (July 16)

1939 William Butler Yeats dies
James Joyce's *Finnegan's Wake* published (previously serialized)

1941 James Joyce dies in Switzerland

1942 Patrick Kavanagh's *The Great Hunger*

1945 John McCormack dies in Dublin

1950 George Bernard Shaw dies

1952 Samuel Beckett's *Waiting for Godot*

BELOW: Beloved of so many of the Irish writers and playwrights of the eary 19th century — the simple fisherfolk of the west of Ireland.